The Up & Running Series from SYBEX

Other titles include Up & Running with:

- **AutoSketch 3**
- **Carbon Copy Plus**
- **DOS 3.3**
- **Flight Simulator**
- **Harvard Graphics**
- **Lotus 1-2-3 Release 2.2**
- **Lotus 1-2-3 Release 3.1**
- **Norton Utilities**
- **PageMaker 4 on the PC**
- **PageMaker on the Macintosh**
- **PC Tools Deluxe 6**
- **PC-Write**
- **PROCOMM PLUS**
- **Q & A**
- **Quattro Pro 3**
- **Quicken 4**
- **ToolBook for Windows**
- **Turbo Pascal 5.5**
- **Windows 3.0**
- **Windows 286/386**
- **WordPerfect Library/Office PC**
- **XTreeGold 2**
- **Your Hard Disk**

Computer users are not all alike.
Neither are SYBEX books.

We know our customers have a variety of needs. They've told us so. And because we've listened, we've developed several distinct types of books to meet the needs of each of our customers. What are you looking for in computer help?

If you're looking for the basics, try the **ABC's** series, or for a more visual approach, select **Teach Yourself**.

Mastering and **Understanding** titles offer you a step-by-step introduction, plus an in-depth examination of intermediate-level features, to use as you progress.

Our **Up & Running** series is designed for computer-literate consumers who want a no-nonsense overview of new programs. Just 20 basic lessons, and you're on your way.

SYBEX Encyclopedias provide a comprehensive reference and explanation of all of the commands, features and functions of the subject software.

Sometimes a subject requires a special treatment that our standard series doesn't provide. So you'll find we have titles like **Advanced Techniques, Handbooks, Tips & Tricks**, and others that are specifically tailored to satisfy a unique need.

You'll find SYBEX publishes a variety of books on every popular software package. Looking for computer help? Help Yourself to SYBEX.

For a complete catalog of our publications:

SYBEX Inc.
2021 Challenger Drive, Alameda, CA 94501
Tel: (415) 523-8233/(800) 227-2346 Telex: 336311
Fax: (415) 523-2373

Up & Running with Grammatik™ *IV 2.0*

■ ■ ■ ■ ■ ■ ■ ■ ■ ■ ■

David J. Clark

SYBEX®

San Francisco ■ Paris ■ Düsseldorf ■ Soest

Acquisitions Editor: Dianne King
Series Editor: Joanne Cuthbertson
Editor: Peter Weverka
Project Editor: Kathleen Lattinville
Technical Editor: Nancy Dannenberg
Word Processors: Ann Dunn, Lisa Mitchell
Book Designer: Ingrid Owen, Helen Bruno
Icon Designer: Helen Bruno
Screen Graphics: Cuong Le
Desktop Production Artist: Helen Bruno
Proofreader/Production Assistant: Rhonda Holmes
Indexer: Ted Laux
Cover Designer: Archer Design
Screen reproductions produced by XenoFont.

XenoFont is a trademark of XenoSoft.

SYBEX is a registered trademark of SYBEX, Inc.

TRADEMARKS: SYBEX has attempted throughout this book to distinguish proprietary trademarks from descriptive terms by following the capitalization style used by the manufacturer.

SYBEX is not affiliated with any manufacturer.

Every effort has been made to supply complete and accurate information. However, SYBEX assumes no responsibility for its use, nor for any infringement of the intellectual property rights of third parties which would result from such use.

Copyright ©1991 SYBEX Inc., 2021 Challenger Drive, Alameda, CA 94501. World rights reserved. No part of this publication may be stored in a retrieval system, transmitted, or reproduced in any way, including but not limited to photocopy, photograph, magnetic or other record, without the prior agreement and written permission of the publisher.

Library of Congress Card Number: 91-65111
ISBN: 0-89588-818-1

Manufactured in the United States of America
10 9 8 7 6 5 4 3 2 1

Acknowledgments

■ ■ ■ ■ ■ ■ ■ ■ ■

I would like to thank Dianne King and Rudolf Langer at SYBEX for giving me the opportunity to write this book, Peter Weverka for his engaging editing, and my co-workers for being patient with me during times of stress. I would also like to thank the helpful and cooperative staff of Reference Software International, the makers of Grammatik IV, particularly Kellie Mecham, Barry Dacus, Susan Eliot, and Suzanne Davies-Pywell.

Special thanks go to my fiancée Janna Hecker for her encouragement and editorial insight.

SYBEX Up & Running Books

Who this book is for

The Up & Running series of books from SYBEX has been developed for committed, eager PC users who would like to become familiar with a wide variety of programs and operations as quickly as possible. We assume that you are comfortable with your PC and that you know the basic functions of word processing, spreadsheets, and database management. With this background, Up & Running books will show you in 20 steps what particular products can do and how to use them.

What this book provides

Up & Running books are designed to save you time and money. First, you can avoid purchase mistakes by previewing products before you buy them—exploring their features, strengths, and limitations. Second, once you decide to purchase a product, you can learn its basics quickly by following the 20 steps—even if you are a beginner.

Contents & structure

The first step usually covers software installation in relation to hardware requirements. You'll learn whether the program can operate with your available hardware as well as various methods for starting the program. The second step often introduces the program's user interface. The remaining 18 steps demonstrate the program's basic functions, using examples and short descriptions.

Special symbols and notes

A clock shows the amount of time you can expect to spend at your computer for each step. Naturally, you'll need much less time if you only read through the step rather than complete it at your computer.

You can also focus on particular points by scanning the short notes in the margins and locating the sections you are most interested in.

In addition, three symbols highlight particular sections of text:

The Action symbol highlights important steps that you will carry out.

The Tip symbol indicates a practical hint or special technique.

The Warning symbol alerts you to a potential problem and suggestions for avoiding it.

We have structured the Up & Running books so that the busy user spends little time studying documentation and is not burdened with unnecessary text. An Up & Running book cannot, of course, replace a lengthier book that contains advanced applications. However, you will get the information you need to put the program to practical use and to learn its basic functions in the shortest possible time.

We welcome your comments

SYBEX is very interested in your reactions to the Up & Running series. Your opinions and suggestions will help all of our readers, including yourself. Please send your comments to: SYBEX Editorial Department, 2021 Challenger Drive, Alameda, CA 94501.

Preface

■ ■ ■ ■ ■ ■ ■ ■

Grammatik IV is the most popular grammar- and style-checking program on the market. Its interactive checking procedure, selection of writing styles, document statistics, and customization features are top-notch. It is available on MS-DOS, Windows, and Macintosh platforms.

This book covers Grammatik IV, Versions 1.0 and 2.0, for the MS-DOS platform specifically, although many of the procedures described are applicable to the Windows and Macintosh versions as well. The book begins with information on program installation, a general description of the user interface, and the basic document checking features of Grammatik IV. It then moves on to Grammatik's extensive customization features and advanced program uses.

Grammatik IV is excellent for correcting errors that your word processor's spelling checker will never catch—errors such as typos that spell the wrong word correctly, incorrect verb tenses, and split infinitives. Beyond that, Grammatik IV can help you improve your writing by analyzing your documents for style as well. It gives you advice about how often you are using the passive voice, and how easy your documents are to understand, and it lets you know when you're using a word that's out-of-date.

Using Grammatik IV in this way gives you a starting point to think about your writing and so become more aware of your own stylistic tendencies, good and bad. The program will help you develop new skills through this awareness. This book is intended to help you become comfortable with the program in as little time as possible, so you can devote more time to better, more effective writing.

Table of Contents

Step 1
Installing
Grammatik *1*

Step 2
The User
Interface *9*

Step 3
Proofing Documents with
Your Word Processor *15*

Step 4
Selecting Files
for Proofing *21*

Step 5
Proofing
Methods *27*

Step 6
Editing Your
Documents *33*

Step 7
Readability
Statistics *43*

Step 8
Analyzing Your
Writing Style *49*

Step 9
Choosing a
Writing Style *57*

Step 10
Setting the Options
to Suit Your Needs *63*

Step 11
Exploring the
Rule Classes *69*

Step 12
Understanding
the Rule Dictionaries *79*

Step 13
Customizing Grammatik
for Your Word Processor *83*

Step 14
Command
Line Options *89*

Step 15
Refining Spelling
Dictionaries *97*

Step 16
How Grammatik
Checks for Errors *103*

Step 17
Customizing
Grammatik's Rules *107*

Step 18
Making Your
Own Rules *115*

Step 19
Defining Complex
Rule Patterns *121*

Step 20
Where Do You
Go from Here? *129*

Installing Grammatik

Before you install Grammatik on your computer, make a backup working copy of the original disk or disks supplied with the software package. Later you will use this working copy of Grammatik when you install the program. This step tells you how to make the backup copies and how to install Grammatik.

MAKING A BACKUP COPY OF GRAMMATIK

How you create the working copy depends on the size and number of floppy drives your computer has.

To make a disk copy of Grammatik with a dual floppy-drive system, turn on your computer and load DOS, if necessary, in the usual manner. (If you have two floppy drives of different types, such as one 3.5" and one 5.25" drive, make your backup copies with the same techniques you would use to make them on a single floppy-drive system. These techniques are described shortly.)

Making backups with two floppy drives

STEP 1

To make copies from a dual floppy-drive system, type the following command:

    DISKCOPY A: B:

and press the Enter, or Return key. When you see the prompt to insert the source and destination disks, insert Grammatik Disk #1 in drive A and a blank disk in drive B. Then press any key. The DISKCOPY command will copy the contents of Grammatik Disk #1 to your blank disk. If you have a 3.5" drive, you have only one program disk to copy, and you can begin installing Grammatik. If you have a 5.25" drive, you have to copy a second disk as well. Remove the first two disks and insert Grammatik Disk #2 in drive A and a second blank disk in drive B. Next, enter the same commands at the DOS prompt you entered to copy the first disk. Now you can start installing Grammatik.

Making backups with a single floppy drive

To make a disk copy of Grammatik with a single floppy-drive system, turn on your computer and load DOS, if necessary, in the usual manner.

From the DOS prompt, type the following command:

    DISKCOPY A: A:

and press the Enter, or Return key. When you see the prompt to insert the source disk, insert Grammatik Disk #1 in the drive and press any key. The program will ask you to insert the destination disk. Remove Grammatik Disk #1 and insert a blank disk in the drive. Then press any key. The DISKCOPY command will copy the contents of Grammatik Disk #1 to your blank disk. If you have a 3.5" drive, you have only one program disk to copy, and you can start installing Grammatik. If you have a 5.25" drive, remove the disk and repeat the procedure to copy Grammatik Disk #2 onto a second blank disk. Now you can begin installing the program.

Now that you have made your copies, store the original disks in a safe place. Always use the backup copies of the Grammatik disks. Floppy disks are subject to wear and tear, and have a finite lifespan. Protect your investment by using the original disks only once.

INSTALLING GRAMMATIK

Grammatik runs best on a hard disk. If you have a two-floppy drive system and no hard disk, see "Floppy Disk Installation" later in this step. This section explains how to install the program on a hard disk.

Installing Grammatik on a Hard Disk

Installing Grammatik IV on a hard disk is fast and simple. Begin by inserting your working copy of Grammatik Disk #1 into drive A. Next, type

    A:

at the DOS prompt and press Enter to log onto drive A. Then type

    INSTALL

You will see an introductory screen. Press any key to continue. (You can abort the installation procedure now or at any time during the installation process by pressing Ctrl-C.) You will be prompted to enter a drive letter; enter the letter of the drive where you want to store Grammatik.

Unless you choose otherwise, Grammatik is loaded by default into a subdirectory called GMK (or G4 if you have Version 1.0) of the drive you specified. Accept this default subdirectory name to avoid unnecessary customization steps.

STEP 1

After you've accepted the subdirectory name (or chosen a new one), the installation program copies the Grammatik program files onto your hard disk. This procedure takes several minutes. If you have 5.25" program disks, you will be prompted to replace Disk #1 with Disk #2.

Next, Grammatik asks you to personalize your copy of the program. Enter your name or your company's name here; it must be between 5 and 47 characters long.

Modifying the AUTO-EXEC.BAT file

Grammatik cannot be loaded from any directory unless the AUTOEXEC.BAT file in the root directory of your boot drive is modified. To modify the AUTOEXEC.BAT file, the installation program prompts you to enter the letter of your boot drive. Assuming you have installed Grammatik on drive C, the program will insert the lines

```
PATH C:\GMK
SET GMK=C:\GMK\
```

into your AUTOEXEC.BAT file. In the case of Version 1.0, it will insert the lines

```
PATH C:\G4
SET GMK4=C:\G4\
```

Grammatik makes a backup copy of your original file under the name AUTOEXEC.OLD. If you want to modify the file yourself, select *N* for No, and edit the AUTOEXEC.BAT file accordingly when you are finished installing Grammatik.

Selecting a Word Processor

Next you will see a list of word processors, as in Figure 1.1. (You will see a slightly different list if you have Grammatik IV 1.0.) Scroll through the list with the cursor keys and find the word processor you want. You can tell which is the currently selected word processor because an asterisk appears to the left of its name.

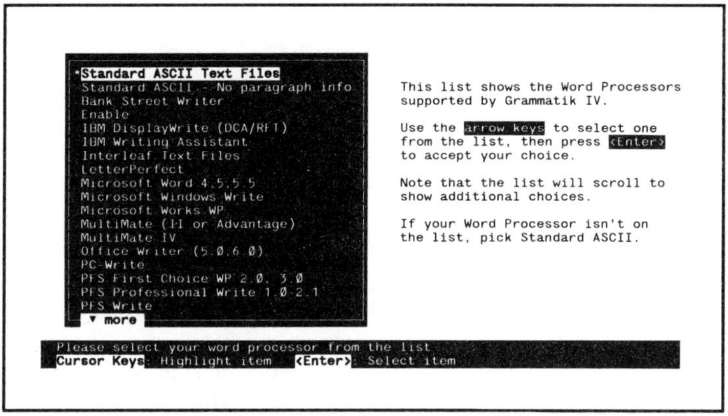

STEP 1

■ *Figure 1.1: The list of word processors supported by Grammatik*

When you've found your word processor, press Enter to select it. If you use more than one word processor, select the one you use most often; you can easily change word processors once you have installed Grammatik. If you are not sure which word processor to use, select the default—Standard ASCII.

Having selected a word processor, you will see some notes that apply to its use and the features available with it. Read this information carefully, and when you're done, press Esc. You'll see the README.TXT file, which contains any late-breaking information about, or corrections to, the Grammatik documentation. Press any key to leave the README.TXT file and finish installing Grammatik IV.

Notes on word processors

Floppy Disk Installation

If you don't have a hard disk, you can still run Grammatik, but you must have a minimum of two 3.5" disk drives, or two 5.25"

Installing Grammatik 5

STEP 1

1.2Mb (high-density) disk drives. Grammatik won't run on a system with two 360K floppy-disk drives and no hard disk.

You can't install either the Master Spelling dictionary (MASTER.-DIC) or the Rule/Help editor (GMKED.EXE in Version 2.0, G4RHED.EXE in Version 1.0) using the floppy disk installation procedures described here. However, depending on how much room is left on your disks, you can install them manually. See "Manual Installation" later in this step to find out how.

Installing Grammatik to floppies

To install Grammatik onto two formatted floppy disks, boot your system with your DOS system disk in drive A. When you see the DOS prompt, remove your DOS system disk from drive A and insert Grammatik IV Disk #1. At the DOS prompt, type

    INSTALL FLOPPY

You will see an introductory screen. Press any key to continue. (You can abort the installation now or at any time during the installation process by pressing Ctrl-C.) You will be prompted to enter a drive letter; enter the letter of the drive where you want to store Grammatik (most likely this will be drive B).

Unless you choose otherwise, Grammatik is loaded by default into the root directory of the drive you specified. Accept the root directory to avoid unnecessary customization steps.

Next the installation program extracts and copies the Grammatik program files onto your floppy disk. This procedure takes several minutes. If you have 5.25" program disks, you will be prompted to replace Disk #1 with Disk #2.

Next, Grammatik asks you to personalize your copy of the program. Enter your name or your company's name here; it must be between 5 and 47 characters long.

Next, you will see a list of word processors (see Figure 1.1). Your list will be slightly different if you have Grammatik IV 1.0. Scroll through the list with cursor keys and find the word processor you want. You can tell which is the currently selected word processor because an asterisk appears to the left of its name. When you've found your word processor, press Enter to select it. If you use more than one word processor, select the one you use most often; you can easily change word processors once you have installed Grammatik. If you are not sure which word processor to use, select the default—Standard ASCII.

Selecting a word processor

Having selected a word processor, you will see some notes that apply to its use and the features available with it. Read this information carefully, and when you're done, press Esc. You'll see the README.TXT file, which contains any late-breaking information about, or corrections to, the Grammatik documentation. Press any key to leave the README.TXT file and finish installing Grammatik IV.

Notes on word processors

Manual Installation

Grammatik IV's program files are shipped to you in compressed format. Suppose you want to install a program file separately because you want it to occupy as little disk space as possible, or you accidentally deleted it and now you have to restore it. You can't simply install a program file by copying it from the original disks. You have to extract program files individually. To do so, insert the Grammatik IV Disk #1 in drive A and type

Extracting program files

    INSTALL EXTRACT

at the DOS prompt. This begins the manual installation procedure. One at a time, Grammatik will describe the use of each of its program files, and it will ask you whether to install each one.

Installing Grammatik 7

To run Grammatik, you must install the following files at minimum:

Grammatik IV, Version 1.0	Version 2.0
G4.WPS	GMK.WPS
G4.EXE	GMK.EXE
G4.DIC	GMK.DIC
G4.HLP	GMK.HLP
G4.PRF	GMK.PRF

The User Interface

Grammatik has a simple and intuitive user interface with a pull-down menu system and dialog boxes. You can execute the common commands with single-key shortcuts and avoid the pull-down menu selections altogether. The Help feature is also available at all times to answer any questions you may have. This step explores the user interface.

STARTING GRAMMATIK

To start Grammatik IV 1.0 from DOS, type

G4

at the DOS prompt and press Enter. To start Grammatik IV 2.0, type

GMK

and press Enter. A brief introductory screen appears, and then you see the Opening screen, as in Figure 2.1.

STEP 2

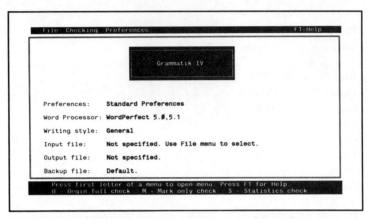

■ *Figure 2.1: The Opening screen*

The Opening screen

At the top of the Opening screen are three menu choices: File, Checking, and Preferences. Select, or "pull down," a menu by pressing the first letter in its name or by moving the cursor to the menu name and pressing Enter. For example, you would press *F* to select, or pull down, the File menu, or else you would move the highlight bar to the File menu with the cursor keys and press Enter.

Mouse support

If you are using Grammatik IV 2.0, and a mouse is installed with your computer, you can use the mouse as well as the keyboard to select a menu. Simply move the mouse pointer—a rectangular bar that moves on screen in conjunction with the movements of your mouse—to the menu you want and click the left button. Users of Version 1.0 should ignore the mouse commands in this book.

Selecting a menu option

Try pressing the Left and Right Arrow keys. Notice how each time you press a key, you select a new menu. To select an option on a menu, press the Up or Down Arrow key to move the cursor to the option you want, and then press Enter. You can select a menu option with the mouse by moving the mouse pointer to the option and clicking the left button. Letters appear to the right of most of the menu options on the File and Checking menus. By pressing one of these letters, you can select and execute the option simultaneously.

You will notice when you browse through the menus that some options are followed by an ellipsis (...). An ellipsis means that when you select the option, a dialog box appears on the screen. Grammatik requires more information before it can execute the command—that's why the dialog box appears. Other options are followed by greater-than symbols (>). When you choose these options, an additional submenu appears to the right of the menu option. Here, you'll have to choose one of several more items.

To leave a menu without selecting an option, press the Esc key. Or, if you have a mouse, you can click the left button while the mouse pointer is not on the menu.

Leaving a menu

The File Menu

Select the File menu by pressing F, by using the right arrow key to move the highlight bar to File and pressing Enter, or by moving the mouse pointer to the word "File" and clicking the left mouse button. Take a moment to look at the options on this menu. You use the File menu to select documents you want to check for grammatical and spelling errors, and to select files with specific sets of proofing preferences. The File menu also allows you to run a DOS command or quit Grammatik. In Version 1.0, you can also specify a path for your spelling dictionary from this menu.

The File menu is for selecting documents

The Checking Menu

Now select the Checking menu by pressing C or by using the cursor keys or mouse. The options on the Checking menu allow you to proof a document for grammatical errors and stylistic problems, perform a statistical analysis of a document, read a document, or remove the corrections made by Grammatik during previous proofing sessions.

Proof documents with the Checking menu

The User Interface   11

Shortcut keystrokes

Because checking documents is the main function of Grammatik, the program was designed so you can bypass the Checking menu and perform common checking tasks directly from the Opening screen. You'll see these common tasks listed at the bottom of the Opening screen (see Figure 2.1). Press B to begin a full, interactive check of your document; press M to mark problem phrasing, allowing you to correct or skip the problem; or press S to do a statistical analysis of your document. You'll learn more about checking documents in Steps 4 and 5.

The Preferences Menu

Customizing Grammatik with the Preferences menu

Select the Preferences menu by pressing P or by using the cursor keys or mouse. Take a quick look at the options on this menu: they allow you to customize Grammatik to your needs. You can choose a writing style, such as Business or Fiction; modify particular rules, which are organized in classes (such as Double negative or Incomplete sentence); select rule dictionaries; select a word processor; turn spell-checking on or off (in Version 2.0); or change Grammatik's screen colors.

The Help Menu

Grammatik provides you with a good on-screen help system. Bring up the Help menu by pressing H or F1, or by clicking on the Help option with the mouse. Grammatik's Help menu will give you advice on the command or procedure you're executing. You can also scroll through Grammatik's Help index to find a specific topic you're interested in.

THE GRAMMATIK TOUR

Grammatik also comes with an introductory tour of its basic features and functions. I recommend taking the tour, as it's a good way to familiarize yourself with the routine tasks you'll encounter in a typical Grammatik work session. The tour provides a sample document to check for grammatical or spelling errors.

To begin the Grammatik tour, log on to the disk drive and directory where your Grammatik program files are located and type

TOUR

at the DOS prompt. Follow the instructions in the Grammatik User's Guide section called "Taking a Guided Tour of Grammatik." It takes from five to fifteen minutes to complete the tour. You can quit the tour at any time by pressing Q.

The User Interface

Proofing Documents with Your Word Processor

Normally you compose a document using your word processor, save the file, exit the word processing program, then run Grammatik, select the document, and check it. But suppose you want to edit the document further. You would have to repeat the process—that is, you would have to save the file, exit your word processor, and run Grammatik all over again. Fortunately, with several of the most common word processors you can switch between your word processor and Grammatik without having to exit one and load the other. You can compose a document, check it in Grammatik, write some more text, and check it again, all without entering and exiting the programs or reselecting the document. This step lists the word processors you can switch back and forth to, describes how to use this switching feature, and gives helpful hints on the word processors that Grammatik supports.

STEP 3

RUNNING GRAMMATIK WITH YOUR WORD PROCESSOR

Word processors supported by Grammatik

If you use one of the word processing programs listed below, you can proof documents inside your word processor. In other words, you can work with Grammatik and your word processor at the same time. If you don't use one of these word processors, skip this step.

- LetterPerfect 2.0 or later (Grammatik IV Version 2.0 only)
- Microsoft Word 5.0 or later
- PFS Professional Write 2.1 or later
- WordPerfect 5 or later
- WordStar 5 or later
- XyWrite III
- XyWrite III Plus (Grammatik IV Version 2.0 only)

Version 1.0

To start Grammatik IV 1.0 and your word processor at the same time and be able to switch between them as you work, type

G4RUNWP

Version 2.0

at the DOS prompt and press Enter. To start Grammatik IV 2.0, type

GMKWP

and press Enter.

Your computer will load Grammatik into memory first, and then your word processor. Go ahead and use your word processor in the normal way. You can access Grammatik with the keystroke combination Alt-G, or a combination of your own, as you will see shortly.

STEP 3

Accessing Grammatik from within Your Word Processor

Alt-G is called a "hot key combination." To check a word-processed file you are currently editing, press Alt-G. Pressing Alt-G saves the current file and starts Grammatik. Soon you'll see the Opening screen, with the word-processed file you were working on automatically selected as the input file. To proof a different file, select the Input file name option on the File menu and choose the new file by scrolling through the list of files with the mouse or arrow keys and pressing Enter. You can also specify the file name by pressing F9, typing the file name, and pressing Enter. Be sure to include the drive and path if the file is not in the current directory.

Starting Grammatik with a hot key combination

You can now perform any Grammatik operations you want. When you quit Grammatik, your word processor is loaded back into memory and the file you had been working on is reopened.

It wouldn't be practical if Alt-G was the only hot key combination you could use. Your word processor might use the Alt-G combination to execute a command, for example. Or you may have designed a useful custom macro that is activated by pressing Alt-G. To access the Goto menu in WordStar 5.0 or later, you have to press Alt-G, so obviously you don't want Alt-G to be the hot key combination that starts Grammatik if you use WordStar.

Changing the hot key combination

Grammatik has anticipated these conflicts by allowing you to change your hot key combination. To do so, load Grammatik from DOS and select the Word processor option on the Preferences menu. A submenu will appear, as in Figure 3.1. Choose the Set G4RUNWP hot key option (Version 1.0) or the Set GMKWP hot key option (Version 2.0).

The screen will display your current hot key combination. Enter a new one. To accept the existing combination, press F10. To accept

Proofing Documents with Your Word Processor **17**

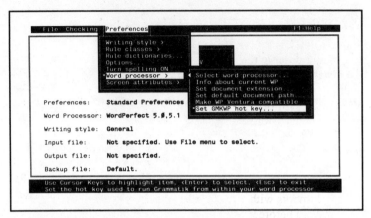

- *Figure 3.1: Changing the hot key combination*

Alt-G, the default, press Esc. However, there are some limitations to what you can select as a hot key combination.

 If you are using WordPerfect 5.0 or 5.1, you must select a letter from A to Z as the one to be pressed in combination with the Alt key. Just enter the letter, not Alt and the letter, when choosing the new hot key combination.

 If you are using a word processor other than WordPerfect, you can select a combination of Alt, Shift, or Ctrl plus a letter or function key. Just make sure that the new combination is not the same as an existing command in your word processor.

 If you loaded Grammatik with the G4RUNWP or GMKWP command when you changed hot key combinations, your new key combination will not become active until you've left the current word processing session.

When you exit your word processor, Grammatik is also closed.

NOTES ON WORD PROCESSORS

Grammatik interacts with each word processing program differently. You should observe the on-screen remarks concerning yours when you install Grammatik. If you didn't read the word processor notes carefully the first time, you can view them again by selecting the Word processor option on the Preferences menu. Next, choose the Info about current WP option on the submenu. Below is a summary of the more important notes about word processors and how they work with the Grammatik hot key combination.

Getting word processor information

If you are using Microsoft 5.0 or later, you cannot delete or add paragraph marks with Grammatik. Be sure to repaginate the document in Word before you print it, as Grammatik edits tend to change page lengths dramatically. Change the hot key combination to one using Shift or Ctrl and a function key.

Microsoft Word 5.0 or later

If you are using a program that has the Word file format as a Save option, such as Ventura Publisher or Microsoft Word for Windows, you will probably have to load the file into Word and save it before Grammatik can successfully read the file.

Programs with Word file formats

After you've edited a document in Grammatik, lines may break incorrectly onscreen in Professional Write. To correct the situation, remove the line break and add a space. Curiously, broken lines are mended when you print the document.

PFS Professional Write 2.1 or later

Don't use WordPerfect's Long Document Name option with Grammatik. If your two documents are open when you press the hot key combination, Grammatik will close both of them and use the one in the active window.

WordPerfect 5 or later

With WordStar 5 or later, make sure the file you are working on is in WordStar's current directory when you press the hot key combination. To print a document you've edited with Grammatik, issue the

WordStar 5 or later

Align rest of document command (Ctrl-QU) from the Layout menu in WordStar.

XyWrite III and XyWrite III Plus

Grammatik only works with one XyWrite open active file, and Grammatik cannot be accessed from the A La Carte menus. One more thing—check print formatting codes, such as underlining, in XyWrite after a Grammatik editing session.

Selecting Files for Proofing

In this step you will learn how to select two types of files in Grammatik—files created by your word processing program to store your document, called "input files," and files you generate inside Grammatik to save sets of preferences, called "preference files."

SELECTING A DOCUMENT TO CHECK

If you are using Grammatik within a word processor, your word-processed document is selected for you automatically. All you have to do is press Alt-G or a hot key combination of your own to proof it. On the other hand, if you loaded Grammatik by itself into DOS (by typing G4 or GMK at the DOS prompt), you will have to select the document before you can proof it.

Suppose you want to check a document you have created with your word processor named LETTER.DOC, for instance. First, you have to specify the file's name for Grammatik. Select the File menu from the Opening screen by pressing F, and press I to select the input file. You will see a dialog box like the one in Figure 4.1. Use the cursor

Selecting an input file

STEP 4

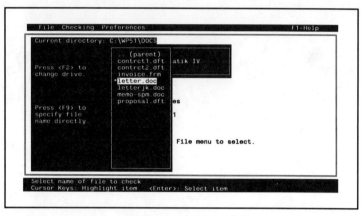

- *Figure 4.1: Selecting a document to check*

keys or mouse to scroll through the list of files and directories until you find LETTER.DOC, and press Enter to select it.

You can also select a file by typing the first letter of its name. Grammatik will move the cursor automatically to the first file name beginning with that letter. Press Enter to select it, or else type the letter again to move the cursor to the next file name that begins with the letter. Another way to select a file name is to press F9 and type in its name. You can specify the drive and path name as well. Be sure to press Enter when you're done.

Grammatik, like many other DOS programs, stores and names backup files under the same file name as the original, but with a different extension. Grammatik uses the extension .G4B for Version 1.0, or .GBK for Version 2.0, for backup files. Because extension names change, it is always a good idea to put the identifying characteristics of the file in the file name, not in the extension. For example, if you write a memo to Sandra P. Michaels, give it the name MEMO-SPM, not MEMO.SPM. That way, the meaningful information about the files will be in both the original file and its backup.

22 *Up & Running with Grammatik*

STEP 4

SELECTING AN OUTPUT FILE

When you proof a document and choose to save your work, Grammatik creates a new file with your corrections. It creates a backup file as well of the uncorrected version of your document. Grammatik assumes you want to save the corrected output file under the same name as the original input file, so it gives the backup—that is, the uncorrected original file—the same name and the extension .G4B for Version 1.0, or .GBK for Version 2.0.

In other words, the default output file, corrected by Grammatik, of your MEMO-SPM.DOC document will be MEMO-SPM.DOC. Meanwhile, the backup file—the original, uncorrected version of the document—will be MEMO-SPM.G4B or MEMO-SPM.GBK, and it will be displayed as such on the Opening screen.

Suppose you want to give the new, corrected version of the document a new name. Select the Output file name option on the File menu. You will see the dialog box shown in Figure 4.2. To enter a new name, press F9 and type the new name. Be sure to identify the file by its name only, not its extension. You can also select an existing file name from the list on the right. If you do, Grammatik will ask whether you are sure you want to overwrite, or erase, the existing file and replace it with your corrected file.

Choosing a new output file name

When you select a new output file name, Grammatik automatically makes your input file the backup file. In other words, suppose you selected MEMO-SPM.DOC as your input file, but you made MEMO2SPM.DOC the output file name. The backup file would be named MEMO-SPM.DOC.

SELECTING A SET OF PREFERENCES

A "preferences file" in Grammatik is one that contains a specific set of options from the Preferences menu. With this feature, you can

STEP 4

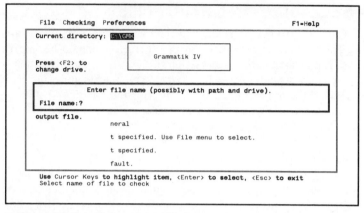

■ *Figure 4.2: Selecting an output file name*

Customizing preferences files

develop a group of option settings, save them in a file, and assign them to particular types of documents.

For example, if you were writing complex technical documents, you would select the Technical writing style and thereby allow yourself longer sentences. You could select these options and save them in a preferences file. That way, when you loaded Grammatik, you could simply make one menu selection and Grammatik would proof your document for its Technical writing style and allow for long sentences.

Making a preferences file

To create a new preferences file, follow these steps:

1. Select any options you want active from the Preferences menu on the Opening screen, pressing **Enter** to activate them. If you are making changes to the options, rule classes, or rule dictionaries, you will need to press F10 to accept the changes.

2. Select the Save preferences file option on the File menu.

3. Press **F9** to create a new preferences file.

STEP 4

4. Type in the file name and press **Enter**. Preferences file names must end with the extension .PRF.

5. You are asked if you want to create a new file. Answer **Y**, for Yes.

6. You are asked if you want to assign a new preferences ID. Enter a description of your set of preferences—it can be up to 31 characters long. Your description will appear on the Opening screen when you select the preferences you are creating.

To make changes to a preferences file, simply select the Get preferences file option on the File menu and choose the file you want to change. Next, make your changes on the Preferences menu and choose the Save preferences file option on the File menu.

Changing a preferences file

To select an existing preferences file to use on your document, choose the Get preferences file option on the File menu. Next, use the mouse or cursor keys to select the correct file from the list of preferences files displayed.

Selecting a preferences file

Selecting Files for Proofing 25

Proofing Methods

One of the unique features of Grammatik is that it provides several different methods for checking your documents. This step describes these methods. You can use only one method or you can use several. The best way to find out which method is best for you is to experiment with all of them.

CHECKING DOCUMENTS FOR GRAMMATICAL AND SPELLING ERRORS

To proof and edit a document as you view it in Grammatik, use the full interactive checking method. To check a document with this method, choose a file to check and then press B (Begin full check) on the Opening screen. You can also select the Begin full interactive option from the Checking menu.   *Full interactive checking*

When Grammatik finds what it thinks is an error in the text, it displays that text on the Error Detection screen, which is shown in Figure 5.1. Notice that Grammatik also offers advice on how to correct the   *The Error Detection screen*

27

STEP 5

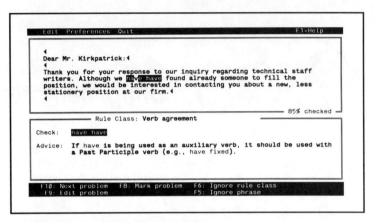

- *Figure 5.1: The Error Detection screen*

problem. At the bottom of the Error Detection screen is a list of options and function keys. You can choose to edit the text (F9), mark the problem for later (F8), replace a word or phrase with one from a list (F2), replace a word and move to the next problem (F3), ignore the phrase for the remainder of the document (F5), ignore that type of grammatical error for the remainder of the document (F6), or have Grammatik search for the next error (F10). During the correction procedure, Grammatik will tell you what percentage of the document has been corrected so far. At the end of the document, a statistical summary is displayed on the screen. We will cover the correction procedure in more detail in Step 6.

Marking errors quickly

Suppose you want to check a long document quickly and go back to review errors later on. In this case, the most effective method is to use one of the Mark Only options. Either press M (Mark only check) from the Opening screen, or select the Mark only, no advice option on the Checking menu. Grammatik will mark suspected problems in your document with a pound sign (#). This is the fastest checking method, but it has one disadvantage—it doesn't say what the problem is, it just marks the problem for you. Once you have marked the errors in your document, you can correct them later with your word processor.

If the pound sign (#) appears in your documents, or if your word processing program uses it as a code, you will want to change the marking character. To do this, select the Options command on the Preferences menu. You will see a dialog box like the one in Figure 5.2. Notice the pound sign in brackets on the top of the right-hand column. This is the marking character. To change this character, use the mouse or cursor keys to move to the marking character option, and press Enter. Next, type in the new character, and press F10 to accept the change.

Changing the marking character

Grammatik also gives you the opportunity to check a document quickly and still receive information about problems, not just a pound sign or customized sign of your own. To check documents this way, select the Mark only, add advice option from the Checking menu. With this method, each problem is marked with a pound sign, and advice about the problem or a description of the error is inserted

Marking errors and getting advice

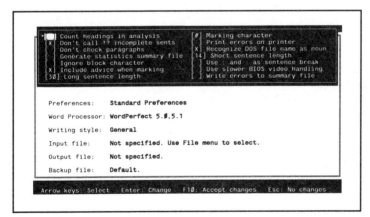

- *Figure 5.2: The Options dialog box*

STEP 5

directly into the text. It appears as a comment in brackets. Once the document is checked, you can view the marked problems and correct them with your word processor.

If you are checking a long document and are limited on disk space, be careful about selecting the Mark only, add advice option. The advice that Grammatik inserts can add quite a bit to the size of your document.

ANALYZING YOUR WRITING

One of the more interesting features of Grammatik is its ability to give an objective numeric and stylistic analysis of your writing. If you are not interested in specific errors but only concerned with how well your document reads, press S (Statistics check) on the Opening screen, or select the Statistics only option on the Checking menu. This will take you directly to the Summary screen. The statistics that appear there will be described in more depth in Step 7.

Reading errors quickly

To save time, Grammatik gives you the option of viewing your errors without being asked to make any changes to the document itself. To check documents this way, select the Read only option on the Checking menu. Now you can view your document in full interactive mode, with the Error Detection screen showing you each problem and suggesting solutions. The Summary screen will appear after you've viewed all the problems, just as it does with other checking methods. Select the Read only option when you want to take an in-depth look at a document and its statistics, or when you want to check your document for errors but not modify it in any way.

Removing Advice

After you've selected the Mark only, add advice option and viewed and edited your document to your satisfaction, you will probably want to remove the advice. So you don't have to search through a

30 *Up & Running with Grammatik*

document and delete the comments with your word processor, Grammatik provides the Remove advice option on the Checking menu. Select this option and Grammatik will find all the advice and delete it for you.

STEP 6

Editing Your Documents

In this step you'll learn how to edit your documents using Grammatik's full interactive checking mode. You'll learn how to correct the errors in your documents as soon as Grammatik uncovers them, and make the appropriate replacements. You'll learn several useful techniques for editing text as well.

In full interactive mode, you can view each problem in its context as it appears in your document, and correct or skip it. The writing process is one of trial and error, and writers often have to recast a sentence several times before they are satisfied with it. The makers of Grammatik took this into account when they designed the program. In full interactive mode, you can play around with sentences until they are just right.

Editing documents on-line

When you check a document, Grammatik stops at each problem, identifies it, and gives you several ways of solving it. You can skip it or mark it for review later on, as you learned in the last step. The program doesn't move on to the next problem until you decide you're ready.

STEP 6

THE ERROR DETECTION SCREEN

You will rewrite and edit all your documents on the Error Detection screen. Once you have selected your document and chosen the Full Interactive checking option, you will see the Error Detection screen. It is shown in Figure 6.1.

The menu bar

At the top of the Error Detection screen is a menu bar much like that on the Opening screen. There are three menus: Edit, Preferences, and Quit. Choose the appropriate menu by selecting it with the mouse or cursor keys, or by pressing the first letter of the menu's name. For example, to select the Edit menu you would press *E*.

The Editing window

The Editing window, which appears in the top half of the Error Detection screen, displays the problem and the text surrounding it. The surrounding text is included to provide you with a contextual reference. Notice the solid, left-pointing arrows. They are there to mark off the end of the line in the word-processed document.

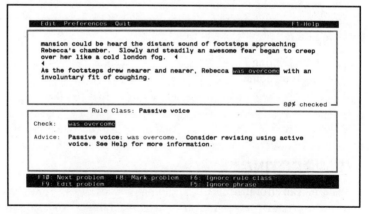

- *Figure 6.1: Editing a document on the Error Detection screen*

STEP 6

The bottom-right corner of the Editing window shows the percentage of the document you have checked so far.

The Writing Problem window on the lower half of the Error Detection screen displays the problem text and gives you explanatory remarks about the problem. If applicable, the Writing Problem window also lists a replacement word or list of words. At the top of this window you see the heading "Rule Class" and the type of problem encountered. For example, in Figure 6.1, Grammatik encountered a "passive voice" error. The Check section displays the problem word or phrase that Grammatik uncovered. The Advice section explains what the problem is and—if it can—suggests a solution. If Grammatik can suggest a replacement word or phrase, it will be shown at the bottom of the Writing Problem window.

The Writing Problem window

It is worthwhile to read what is in the Advice section carefully, as this section can give you useful insights into your own writing. For example, the Advice section will alert you when you use the passive voice, a common problem among writers. If the Advice section discovers the same mistake time and time again, you'll know which part of your writing to work on.

Below the Writing Problem window is a list of function keys followed by brief command descriptions. The function key commands are the same as the options on the Edit menu. Grammatik lists the function key commands at the bottom of the screen so you can execute Edit menu commands quickly.

Function key commands

CORRECTING ERRORS IN THE TEXT

To correct an error that Grammatik has caught, press *E* or select Edit with the mouse or cursor keys. You will see the Edit menu, shown in Figure 6.2.

Editing Your Documents 35

STEP 6

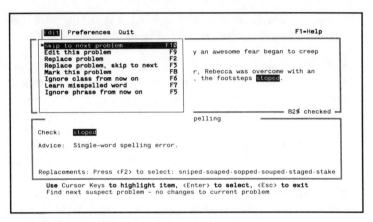

- *Figure 6.2: The Edit menu*

Not all of the options on the Edit menu are relevant to every problem Grammatik encounters in your documents. For this reason, options don't appear on the Edit menu if they aren't applicable to a particular problem. For instance, if you don't have Grammatik's spell checker turned on, you will not see the Learn misspelled word option on the Edit menu. The same is true of the function keys displayed at the bottom of the Error Detection screen.

Skipping to the next problem

If Grammatik has identified a problem word or phrase that you want to keep intact, select the Skip to next problem option, or press F10. Pressing F10 tells Grammatik to move to the next problem on the Error Detection screen.

Correcting a problem

Suppose the problem requires more than a simple replacement, as the split infinitive in Figure 6.3 does. In this case, select the Edit this problem option, or press F9. The cursor will move to the problem word or phrase inside the Editing window.

Insert and Overtype modes

Notice how, in Figure 6.3, the word "Insert" appears at the top of the screen. This means that any characters you type in the Editing

36 *Up & Running with Grammatik*

STEP 6

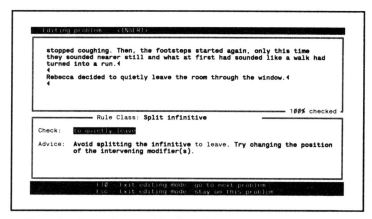

- *Figure 6.3: Correcting a problem by editing*

window will push existing characters to the right. If you prefer to type over the existing characters, you can switch to Overtype mode by pressing the Ins key. The Ins key is a toggle switch—you can press it to switch back and forth from Overtype to Insert mode. The Ins key and other keys and key combinations for editing text in the Editing window are listed below.

Del	Deletes the character at the cursor.
Backspace	Deletes the character to the left of the cursor.
↑	Moves the cursor up one line.
↓	Moves the cursor down one line.
←	Moves the cursor left one character.
→	Moves the cursor right one character.
Ctrl-←	Moves the cursor left one word.
Ctrl-→	Moves the cursor right one word.
Ctrl-L	Deletes the line.

Text editing keys

Editing Your Documents 37

STEP 6

Ins	Toggles between Insert and Overtype mode.
PgUp	Moves the cursor up one screen.
PgDn	Moves the cursor down one screen.
Home	Moves the cursor to the beginning of the line.
Home Home	Moves the cursor to the top of the screen.
Home Home Home	Moves the cursor to the beginning of the document.
End	Moves the cursor to the end of the line.
End End	Moves the cursor to the bottom of the screen.
End End End	Moves the cursor to the end of the document.

Let's look at an example of how to edit text. To correct the split infinitive in Figure 6.3, you would have to change "to quietly leave the room" to "to leave the room quietly." To do this you would follow these steps:

1. Press F9 or select the Edit this problem option on the Edit menu. Grammatik moves the cursor to the *t* in the word "to."
2. Press Ctrl-→ three times to move the cursor to the beginning of the word "quietly."
3. Press the Del key eight times to delete the word "quietly."
4. Press Ctrl-→ three times to move to the end of the word "room."
5. Press the → key twice to move past the word "room."
6. Type in the word "quietly."

38 *Up & Running with Grammatik*

When you are through making changes, leave the Editing window and save your changes by pressing F10. Grammatik will go to the next problem.

Saving your corrections

Alternatively, you can leave the Editing window but remain on the same problem. To do so, press Esc.

The Select a replacement option appears on the Edit menu when Grammatik can suggest a single replacement word as a solution to a problem. For example, if you misspelled a word or typed the same word twice by mistake, you will see the Select a replacement option. To invoke this command, press F2. If more than one possible replacement is available, a list of replacement words appears on the screen. Scroll through the list with the mouse or cursor keys, find the word you want, and press Enter or click on the left mouse button to select it.

Selecting a replacement word

However, if the word you intended to spell is not on the list, press Esc to abandon the select replacement option, and press F9 to enter the Editing window and make the necessary changes yourself.

When Grammatik misidentifies a word as misspelled, such as a name or other proper noun, you can bypass the word by press-ing F10. Grammatik will simply move to the next problem.

In Version 2.0, you can use the Replace problem, skip to next option or press F3 to select a word from the replacement list and go directly to the next problem. With this option, you don't have to press F10 to move to the next problem: Grammatik takes you there automatically.

In order to make corrections in your documents, you might have to leave what you're doing and consult another page to find out, for example, whether the heroine of your novel has brown or blue eyes. Or, you might want to stop and think for a while about how to re-phrase a passage of text. Either way, to make sure you come back to the problem later, you can mark it. Select the Mark this problem

Marking problems for later consider- ation

Editing Your Documents **39**

option, or press F8. This way, you can view the problem and edit it later with your word processor, using Grammatik's marking character to locate it. (Marking characters were discussed in the previous step.)

Bypassing Misspelled Words

Adding words to Grammatik's dictionary

Grammatik's dictionary contains most common words, but gaps in its vocabulary appear from time to time. Moreover, Grammatik cannot recognize the proper nouns, names, or technical terms you may use. To keep the program from stopping on these words when it proofs your documents, you can add them to Grammatik's dictionary. Press F7 to select the Learn misspelled word option (called "Learn spelling word" in Version 1.0), and Grammatik will bypass the word the next time it encounters it.

The Learn misspelled word option only appears if the spell checker is on.

When to use the spell checker

In Grammatik IV Version 2.0, the spell checker (referred to by the program as "single-word spelling") is normally turned on, and Grammatik checks your documents for spelling errors as well as grammatical and stylistic problems. Grammatik's spell checker is quite good, but you may prefer to check your spelling with your own word processor's spell checker. For example, if you are in the medical or legal fields, you likely use a spelling dictionary with specialized vocabulary, and you'll want to check word spellings in your word processor, not with Grammatik.

Turning version 2.0's spell checker off

To turn the spelling feature off in Grammatik Version 2.0, select the Turn spelling OFF option on the Preferences menu. The Preferences menu that appears at the top of the Error Detection screen is an abbreviated version of the Preferences menu on the Opening screen—only the Word processor and Screen attributes options are left out. To choose the Preferences menu, press *P* or select it with the mouse or cursor keys.

The spell checker is normally turned off in Grammatik IV Version 1.0. To turn it on, select the Rule classes option on the Preferences menu on the Opening screen. Next, select the Mechanical option. Use the cursor keys to move the asterisk to the Single-word spelling option, and press Enter. An *X* will appear to show that the option is now active. Press F10 to accept the modification or press Esc to abort the change. To turn the option back off, repeat the procedure.

Turning Verrsion 1.0's spell checker on

Ignoring Grammatik Grammar or Style Rules

Grammatik groups the errors it finds into categories called "rule classes." (Rule classes are explained in more depth in Step 11.) When the program suggests a change, it does so on the basis of a rule. But suppose the rule doesn't suit you? For example, suppose you were writing a technical or academic document and you considered the passive voice acceptable or even preferable. Grammatik would still identify passive sentences and ask you to consider rephrasing them, which might prove tedious after a while. Fortunately, you can press F6 to select the Ignore class from now on option. This way, when the problem occurs, Grammatik will ignore it. In our example, it would ignore passive voice occurrences for the rest of the document.

The Ignore class option

You will select the Ignore class from now on option more frequently to ignore the suggestions Grammatik gives you for stylistic improvements. Rarely should you let a grammatical error stand.

Bypassing Phrases

Suppose an ungrammatical word or phrase appears throughout your document and you don't want to change it. To have Grammatik ignore the phrase, press F5 to invoke the Ignore phrase from now on option.

The Ignore phrase form now on option

STEP 6

The Show parts of speech info option

Learning about Grammar

There is an additional feature on the Edit menu, the Show parts of speech info option. Activate this option by pressing F4, and Grammatik will show you how it breaks down the sentences displayed on your screen into parts of speech—nouns, verbs, adjectives, etc. This feature can be useful if you are not sure of the parts of speech and you want to understand why Grammatik offers advice on a given problem.

Readability Statistics

In order to detect and identify grammatical errors, Grammatik identifies and classifies the different parts of speech in a document. With this information already at hand, Grammatik can tabulate statistics that give you an objective idea about the level of complexity—and readability—of your document.

No computer program can analyze the complexity of human thought expressed in language and gauge that complexity effectively on a numeric index. Clarity of exposition doesn't necessarily bear a close correspondence to the simplicity of a sentence's structure. However, Grammatik's readability scores can be useful because they provide you with a clear indicator of the trends that mark your writing style.

How readability statistics help you

If you tend to write long sentences with many digressions, as I do, the readability statistics will tell you that your sentences are longer than average. Academic philosophers may need to write long sentences to describe complex ideas—that's fine. But business correspondents who write long sentences should consider trying a simpler, more direct

STEP 7

approach. Use the readability statistics as guidelines—they weren't meant to be like the letter grades given to English compositions.

This step tells you how to read the Summary screen that contains statistics about your document. You'll learn how these statistics can be of benefit in improving your writing style.

EXPLORING THE SUMMARY SCREEN

After you finish checking a document, you see the readability statistics displayed on the Summary screen, as in Figure 7.1. You can obtain the readability statistics without performing a full interactive check by selecting the Statistics check option on the Opening screen, or by selecting the Statistics only option on the Checking menu after you've selected an input file to check.

The menu bar

First, look at the menu bar on the Summary screen. The File menu offers an abbreviated set of commands similar to those on the File menu of the Opening screen. The Statistics menu lets you access

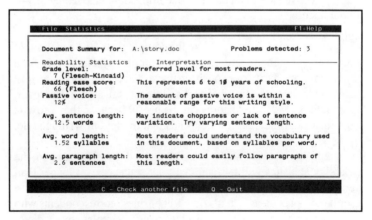

- *Figure 7.1: The Summary screen*

44 *Up & Running with Grammatik*

STEP 7

more statistical information about your document. The features on the Statistics menu are discussed in Step 8.

The name of the document is displayed at the top of the screen, as is a count of the problems detected in the document.

The remainder of the Summary screen is divided into two columns titled "Readability Statistics" and "Interpretation." The first column gives you the scores on the various indexes, and the second gives you an explanation of what these scores mean. The indexes are explained below. The precise formulas used to derive these scores are listed in the *Grammatik IV User's Guide*, if you're curious.

Grade level

The Grade level index averages out the number of words per sentence and the number of syllables per word to determine how complex your document is. Finally, it determines the grade level of readers who could read your document comfortably. The sample document in Figure 7.1 has a grade level of 7 and could be theoretically understood by a reader with a seventh grade education. Grammatik has determined that this score is the "preferred level for most readers." The target range of seventh through tenth grade is often sought for writing intended for a general audience. Many newspapers target an eighth grade reading level for the vocabulary of their articles.

Reading ease score

The Reading ease score index uses a scale of 0–100 to show reading ease, 0 being the most difficult and 100 being the easiest. Standard reading difficulty is between 60 and 70. These scores also correspond to years of schooling. Our sample document has a score of 66, which puts it in the standard range, and makes it ideal for readers with "6 to 10 years of schooling."

A very common weakness in formal writing is the excessive use of the passive voice. "The spurious report was issued by her" is an example of the passive voice. "She issued the spurious report" is preferable, since

STEP 7

it uses the active voice. Excessive use of the passive voice makes simple declarative statements sound abstract. Scientists and journalists often use the passive voice to make their interpretation of facts appear completely objective. They want to show how far they have distanced themselves from their conclusions.

There is nothing wrong with casting a sentence in the passive voice when the agent of the action is less important than the action itself. For example, there's nothing wrong with the sentence "The wallet was found by a passerby." Here we are interested in the fate of the wallet, not the person who found it. However, if the next sentence tells us that "The wallet was not reported lost by anyone," the passage becomes unnecessarily dreary, as two passive sentences appear in sequence.

In our example in Figure 7.1, the passive voice was used 12 percent of the time—a reasonable amount for general writing. Notice that the interpretation says that this amount is reasonable "for this writing style." Some types of writing, such as technical writing, allow for more use of the passive voice.

The next three averages—sentence, word, and paragraph length—help identify stylistic and organizational difficulties.

Average sentence length

In the example, the average sentence length is only 12.5 words. One simple sentence, like this one, with only twelve words, is fine. However, if all of your sentences are this short, your document can become difficult to read, as the interpretation in Figure 7.1 points out.

Average word length

Not all polysyllabic words are complicated, but averaging out the number of syllables per word gives you a rough indication of how complex your vocabulary is. Of course, there are plenty of short but rare words, and writers who use a lot of long words don't necessarily have large vocabularies. For example, more readers would be able to understand "His statement was long-winded" than "His statement

STEP 7

was prolix." Yet it is generally best to avoid using a long word if you can find an acceptable short word to use in its place.

The paragraph length average indicates how well you have organized and presented your ideas. If your paragraphs have too many sentences, for instance, they may be difficult for readers to understand.

Average paragraph length

Analyzing Your Writing Style

The readability statistics discussed in the previous step, which are displayed every time you check a document, provide you with general information about your writing. But what if you want to analyze your writing style even more closely? Grammatik provides you with advanced tools for doing just that. And the more time you spend customizing the program and exploring its capabilities, the more sensitive and useful these tools become. This step shows you how to view additional statistics and document comparisons.

DOCUMENT STATISTICS

Figure 8.1 shows the Statistics menu of the Summary screen. Reach this screen by selecting the Full interactive option, Mark only option, or the Statistics only option from the Checking menu on the Opening screen. The Statistics screen appears after you've checked the document. The first option on the Statistics menu is "Document statistics." Select this option and you will see an in-depth analysis of the statistics on the Summary screen, as in Figure 8.2.

In-depth analysis of the statistical summary

STEP 8

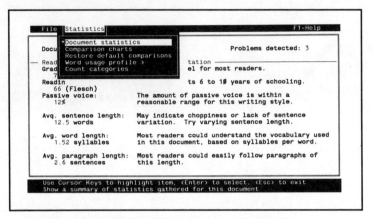

- *Figure 8.1: The Statistics menu on the Summary screen*

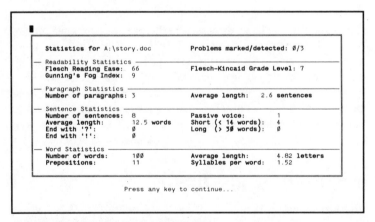

- *Figure 8.2: Viewing document statistics*

Readability statistics

The first group of statistics are identical to those on the Summary screen. You'll see the readability indexes—the Flesch Reading Ease score and the Flesch-Kincaid Grade Level. You'll also see the Gunning's Fog Index, a formula that averages the number of words per sentence and the number of syllables per word. The resulting score, which is 9 in Figure 8.2, tells you the grade level at which your document can be comfortably read.

The remaining sets of statistics give you information about smaller units—paragraphs, sentences, words, syllables, and letters.

Paragraph Statistics

The Paragraph Statistics section lists the number of paragraphs in your document and the average paragraph length in words. Some writers, such as journalists, require short paragraphs, where others need to improve an abrupt or choppy style caused by one- or two-sentence paragraphs. Either way, the Paragraph Statistics section can help you tell if you are succeeding in the writing style you chose.

Sentence Statistics

The Sentence Statistics section lists the

- number of sentences in your document,
- the average sentence length in words,
- the number of sentences ending with an exclamation point (!),
- the number of sentences ending with a question mark (?),
- the number of sentences in the passive voice,
- the number of short sentences, and
- the number of long sentences.

Many writers use the exclamation point too often in an attempt to show enthusiasm. However, using the exclamation point too often makes the writing sound hysterical and can annoy the reader. Check the number of exclamation points in your document to see if you have this problem.

Another writing problem is overuse of the question mark. Some writers, enamored with the technique of beginning a paragraph with

Analyzing Your Writing Style

a question, start every paragraph with one. Conversely, you may find an article too dry and want to pepper your prose with questions to engage and involve the reader. Checking the number of question marks helps you with both of these problems.

For its purposes, Grammatik has determined that the number of words in a long sentence is 30, and the number of words in a short sentence is 14. These numbers vary depending on the writing style you have selected. You can change the number of words that constitute a long or short sentence. Customize the number from the Options selection on the Preferences menu.

Word Statistics

The Word Statistics section lists the number of words in your document, their average length in letters and syllables, and how many of them are prepositions. A preposition is a linking word like "at," "on," "through," or "by."

COMPARISON CHARTS

You can compare your writing against masters

After you've seen all the numbers explained above, you may want something more tangible than an abstract numerical benchmark with which to compare your documents. For this reason, Grammatik lets you compare your documents with three very different types of writing: Lincoln's "Gettysburg Address," an Ernest Hemingway short story, and a life insurance policy.

Lincoln and Hemingway wrote direct and effective prose. Lincoln's stirring speech at Gettysburg has become a model of clarity of exposition, and is taught to most school children. Hemingway's fiction is also prized for its clarity, but also its simplicity and directness. By comparing your writing against the life insurance policy, you can see if you are being too formal in style, which is not what you want to do, for example, if you are writing an informal letter. On the other hand, if you are writing legal and contractual documents, the life insurance policy can serve as an excellent benchmark.

STEP 8

Select the Comparison charts option on the Statistics menu. The bar charts you see on the screen give you a pictorial comparison of your document to the examples. The bar charts are shown in Figure 8.3. This screen is the first of two.

The first screen shows how your document compares to the other three on the Flesch Reading Ease Score and Flesch-Kincaid Grade Level indexes. By pressing Enter, you can see a second screen with charts comparing the average number of sentences per paragraph, average words per sentence, and average letters per word in your document with the samples. You can also compare your prepositions as a percentage of the total words with those in the samples.

Reading the charts

Customizing the Comparison Charts

What if you don't care for Hemingway's writing and you'd like to use another writing example as a benchmark? Don't worry. You are not limited to the three samples provided by Grammatik. You can choose any document as a standard by which to compare your work.

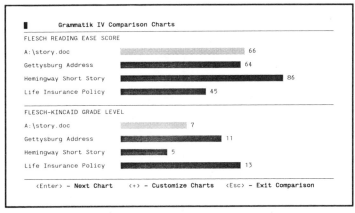

- *Figure 8.3: The first Comparison Chart screen*

Analyzing Your Writing Style 53

STEP 8

To customize the comparison chart and choose a new comparison document,

1. Select a replacement document as the input file by bringing up the File menu on the Opening screen.
2. Press **S** (Statistics only) to run a statistics check of the document.
3. Select the Comparison charts option on the Statistics menu.
4. Press the **plus sign** (+) to customize the charts.
5. Select which of the three standard files you want to replace by typing 1, 2, or 3, the number to which it corresponds.
6. Enter a description up to 23 characters long and press **Enter**.

Press Esc if you decide not to change comparison documents after all, and don't worry—you can always restore the original samples. You can replace all three comparison documents with your own standards by repeating the steps above.

Restoring default comparisons

To retrieve the original comparison documents, select the Restore default comparisons option on the Statistics menu (see Figure 8.1). The original comparisons will be in effect the next time you load Grammatik.

WORD USAGE PROFILE

Grammatik compiles a list of all the words in your document and the frequency with which you've used each word. This list has many useful applications. For example, you can tell if you are using one word or type of word too often. Or, if you are writing marketing or sales brochures and you want to include a certain product name or catch phrase often, the list will tell you if you are not using a word often enough.

Select the Word usage profile option on the Statistics menu (see Figure 8.1) to examine your choice of words. From the submenu that appears, you can select different kinds of word lists. For simple on-screen viewing, select one of the three sort options, Alphabetical order, Most frequent first, or Least frequent first. Each displays a list on your screen through which you can scroll to view all the words in your document.

Word lists

You can print a word list or send its contents to an ASCII disk file, or view it on the screen. To do so, select the Interactive profile mode option on the Word Usage Profile menu.

The Word Usage Profiler is also available as an external DOS program that you can use without having to run Grammatik itself. To run the Profiler, type

GMKPROF

at the DOS prompt for Version 1.0, or type

G4PROF

for Version 2.0.

The Count categories option on the Statistics menu (see Figure 8.1) is used to count elements of your document that you have requested Grammatik to keep track of. However, to make use of this option you must have customized the program with the Rule and Help Editor. This is covered in detail in Step 19.

Count categories

Analyzing Your Writing Style **55**

Choosing a Writing Style

Writing styles differ from person to person, not only according to the writer's taste and sensibility, but also according to the type of writing being undertaken. For example, a technical document calls for an entirely different writing style than a love letter does. For this reason, Grammatik has created five sets of rules, each of which governs one of five typical writing styles. The program lets you enable or disable various rule classes and rule dictionaries. This way, you can grade your document with rules that are appropriate for the writing style you're trying for. You can also redefine the long sentence and short sentence size to suit your writing style. The Writing style option is a quick way to customize the program for your needs.

CHANGING WRITING STYLES

To choose a style, go to the Opening screen and select the Writing style option on the Preferences menu. You will see the submenu shown in Figure 9.1. From this menu you can choose one of six styles: General, Business, Technical, Fiction, Informal, and Custom. These styles are described below.

Selecting a writing style

STEP 9

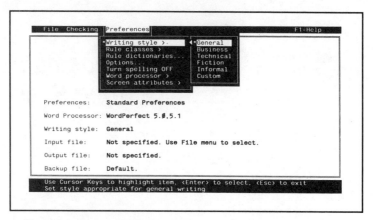

* *Figure 9.1: Grammatik's writing styles*

General style

General is the default writing style—it is in effect when you load Grammatik for the first time and it remains in effect until you select another style. With the General style, a fairly strict one, almost all the rules are turned on. Thirty words is considered a long sentence and fourteen is considered a short one. Only the gender specificity rule class is turned off with the General writing style. The gender specificity rule class warns you when you are using gender-specific nouns, such as "chairman," or condescending phrases, such as "the weaker sex."

The Single-word spelling option, which simply checks your document for correct spelling, is also turned off in Grammatik IV Version 1.0, as it is in all writing styles. You can turn it on by choosing the Rules classes option in the Mechanical dialog box under the Preferences menu. In Version 2.0, single-word spelling is turned on in all writing styles.

Business style

Business correspondence is a formal affair. Therefore, the Business writing style is the strictest. It has all rules and dictionaries turned on.

The long sentence setting is 24 words and the short sentence setting is 12.

With the Technical writing style, all rule classes are turned on except for jargon. The Technical writing style permits jargon, because some jargon words that are commonly misused in standard writing, such as the verb "to interface," are strictly defined technical terms, and are appropriate in their original environments. The Technical writing style allows for a long sentence setting of 28 words and a short sentence setting of 12 words.

Technical writing style

The Fiction style allows you much more latitude, since much of fiction is on the experimental edge of modern prose. Besides, reproducing dialogue requires looser rules, because spoken English is also looser. Many rules appropriate for general nonfiction, business, or technical writing would be annoying or irrelevant in fiction. The long sentence setting with the Fiction style is 30 words, the short sentence setting is 14.

Fiction style

The rules disabled for the Fiction writing style include Cliche, Foreign, Gender Specific, Incomplete Sentences, Informal or Colloquial, Split Infinitive, and Vague Adverb. Explanations of these rule classes and dictionaries are found in Steps 11 and 12.

The Informal style allows for the most latitude of all. It approximates spoken English in its rules. The long sentence setting with the Informal style is 30 words, the short sentence setting is 14.

Informal style

A list of the rules disabled for the Informal writing style follows. Look at this long list carefully. It is included so you can see the various—and numerous—writing style rules in Grammatik.

Recognize DOS as Noun, Strict Rules Dictionary, Business Rules Dictionary, Archaic, Cliche, Ellipsis Mark, Foreign, Gender Specific, Incomplete Sentences, Informal or Colloquial,

Choosing a Writing Style 59

STEP 9

Jargon, Long Sentence, Long-Winded, Number Style, Overstated or Pretentious, Paragraph Problem, Passive Voice, Redundant, Relative Pronoun, Split Infinitive, Trademark, Unbalanced Pairs, and Vague Adverb.

CREATING A CUSTOMIZED WRITING STYLE

You can create your own customized writing style in Grammatik. Simply select Custom from the Writing style options on the Preferences menu. You will see the dialog box in Figure 9.2. From here you can press Esc and enable or disable any of the options on the Preferences menu. These changes will remain in effect for your current work session. When you quit Grammatik by selecting Quit from the File menu, you will be asked if you want to save the changes you have made to the preferences. Answer Y to save the changes and you will have a customized style for your next checking session.

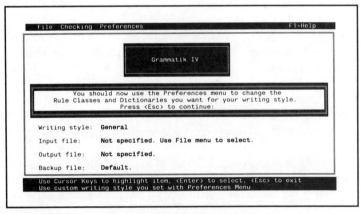

- *Figure 9.2: Designing a customized writing style*

STEP 9

Let's try experimenting with the Custom writing style option. Suppose you wanted to check the grammar and punctuation in your documents but not the spelling because you do that with your word processor.

1. Select Writing style from the Preferences menu on the Opening screen.
2. Select the Custom option. You will see the dialog box in Figure 9.2. Press **Esc** to continue.
3. To turn off the style rules, select the **Rule** classes option from the Preferences menu.
4. Because we want to have Grammatik check for all grammatical errors, leave the Grammatical and Mechanical options alone for now. Select the Style option.
5. Notice how all the style options are enabled by default in the Custom writing style. Let's turn them off. Press **Enter** and the *X* disappears from the Archaic option—it's been disabled.
6. Use the cursor keys or mouse to move to each option and disable it until all style options have been disabled.
7. Press **F10** to accept the changes (or press Esc to abandon them).
8. Now we'll turn the spelling checker off. If you have Version 2.0, simply select the **Turn** spelling OFF option from the Preferences menu and press **Enter**.

    If you have Version 1.0, select the Mechanical option. Use the cursor keys or mouse to move to the Single-word spelling option. If it is enabled—that is, if it is displaying an *X*—disable it by pressing **Enter**.

Choosing a Writing Style

STEP 9

9. Press **F10** to accept the changes.
10. Now select **Q**uit from the File menu to leave Grammatik. You will be asked if you want to save the changes made to the preferences.
11. Press **Y** to save them for your custom writing style—they will be available for your next session.

STEP 10

Setting the Options to Suit Your Needs

Some of Grammatik's features don't fit in the categories of rule classes or dictionaries. The features on the Options submenu of the Preferences menu allow you to make decisions about the way Grammatik checks a file. For example, you can choose whether to include headings in the document analysis, whether to count phrases ending in semicolons as sentences, and so on. This step explains each of these options and how to turn them on or off.

MODIFYING THE OPTIONS LIST

To change the way Grammatik IV reads a document, change the features on the Options list. To view the Options list, select Options on the Preferences menu of the Opening screen. You will see the Options list shown in Figure 10.1. (The Options list looks somewhat different in Grammatik IV Version 1.0; the differences are explained throughout this step.)

Most of the options are toggle switches. That is, you use the same key, Enter, to switch them on or off. An option is enabled if an *X* is

STEP 10

```
*[ ] Count headings in analysis          [#] Marking character
[X] Don't call !? incomplete sents.      [ ] Print errors on printer
[ ] Don't check paragraphs               [X] Recognize DOS file name as noun
[ ] Generate statistics summary file     [14] Short sentence length
[ ] Ignore block character               [ ] Use ; and : as sentence break
[X] Include advice when marking          [ ] Use slower BIOS video handling
[30] Long sentence length                [ ] Write errors to summary file


Preferences:     Standard Preferences
Word Processor:  WordPerfect 5.0,5.1
Writing style:   General
Input file:      Not specified. Use File menu to select.
Output file:     Not specified.
Backup file:     Default.

Arrow keys: Select   Enter: Change   F10: Accept changes   Esc: No changes
```

- *Figure 10.1: The Options list*

displayed within the brackets beside it. Look at Figure 10.1. The options with an *X* or other characters inside their brackets are enabled by default.

Enabling and disabling options

To enable an option, you have to select it first. You can tell when an option is selected because an asterisk appears to the left of the brackets. To select an option, move the asterisk beside it using the mouse or arrow keys. Press Enter and an *X* appears. To disable an option, select it in the same manner and press Enter. The *X* will disappear. You can change as many options as you want on the Options list. Once you have changed all the options you want, press F10 to save the changes. If you want to cancel the changes you made, press Esc and type N.

OPTION DESCRIPTIONS

Let's look at the options one by one. Where there are differences between Versions 1.0 and 2.0, they will be explained.

STEP 10

When the Capitalize words proper nouns option (available only in Version 1.0) is turned on, capitalized words in the middle of a sentence are assumed to be proper nouns, or names. To turn this option off, press Enter.

The Check "leading" punctuation option (available only in Version 1.0) warns you when you are starting a sentence with punctuation. Of course, the only punctuation mark that can begin a sentence is the quotation mark ("). This option can be useful for finding out how much of a fiction work is dialogue. Press Enter to turn this option on.

Turn the Count headings in analysis option on to include headings, such as section titles, in your statistical analysis. This option is useful, for example, in technical documents, which usually include a lot of headings. By pressing Enter and turning this option on, you can tell if you've included too many or too few headings.

Count headings in analysis

Grammatik assumes that phrases ending with an exclamation point or question mark are complete sentences. By disabling the Don't call !? incomplete sentences option, you can have Grammatik call these sentences to your attention. Disable this option by pressing Enter.

Don't call !? incomplete sentences

The Don't check paragraphs option is called "No paragraph checking" in Version 1.0. If you enable this option, Grammatik will skip errors like "one sentence paragraph." Bear in mind that the program will also not gather statistical information on paragraphs. If you do have a lot of one-sentence paragraphs in your work, you might consider disabling this option. That way, you'll save time during document checks.

Don't check paragraphs

The computer algorithms that Grammatik uses to locate mistakes range from the simple to the complex. To detect misspelled words, Grammatik just compares the words in your document with those in

Setting the Options to Suit Your Needs **65**

STEP 10

its dictionary. However, some algorithms for finding grammatical errors are much more subtle. The more meticulous Grammatik is in identifying all grammatical rules, the more likely it will inadvertently mistake a correct phrase for an incorrect one. If you find this kind of meticulousness annoying, press Enter to disable the Find more false problems option. This option is only available in Version 1.0.

Generate statistics summary file

By enabling the Generate statistics summary file option, you can have Grammatik generate a disk file containing the readability statistics for each of your documents. The file will have the same file name as your document, but its file extension will be .SUM. For instance, if your file is called REPORT.DOC, the readability statistics file will be named REPORT.SUM. If you want to keep a record of your summaries, enable this option.

Ignore block character

The Ignore block character option is very useful if your document contains foreign language excerpts, computer programming source code, or other non-English text. To select this option, press Enter. You will be asked to specify a block character. When you write your document, insert the block character at the beginning and end of each section you want Grammatik to skip. The program will not attempt to check anything between the block characters. Choose a character, such as an asterisk (*) or ampersand (&), not found in the regular body of your document.

Include advice when marking

The Include advice when marking option is normally enabled. As you know, Grammatik inserts its corrective advice during the checking process, and the advice appears in text and is enclosed by pound signs (#) if you elect to mark a problem. If you don't want the advice inserted into the document, press Enter to disable this option.

Long sentence length

Grammatik sets a standard for the number of words in what it considers the longest permissible sentence and the shortest permissible sentence. It warns you to consider changing the length of a sentence that is too long or too short. For most styles, the long sentence length is set at 30 words. To change this setting, select the Long sentence length option and enter the number of words you think should be permissible in a long sentence.

Grammatik normally uses the pound sign (#) to enclose advice or to mark errors in your documents. If you need the pound symbol for other purposes, or if it is used as a code by your word processor, you can make another character the marking character. Select the Marking character option and enter the new character. It will be displayed on the Options list.

Marking character

The Print errors on printer option sends all errors and advice to your printer. If you enable this option, make sure your printer has paper, is connected properly, and is online before you begin checking a document. When you're done, you'll get a printed readout of all errors and advice. You can study the readouts to see what kind of errors you're making in your writing.

Print errors on printer

The Quoted items "literal" nouns option, available only in Grammatik IV Version 1.0, tells the program that single words in quotes are nouns. This is useful when you are discussing specialized vocabulary or foreign words (because they tend to describe nouns). To disable this option, press Enter.

When enabled, the Recognize DOS file name as noun option tells Grammatik that character strings such as LETTER.TXT are DOS file names with extensions. With this option on, the program won't mark character strings as punctuation mistakes. Leave this option on if your writing includes PC file names.

Recognize DOS file name as noun

The Short sentence length option sets the standard for the shortest permissible sentence, which is 14 words for most styles. To change this standard, enter the number of words you think the shortest permissible sentence should comprise.

Short sentence length

STEP 10

For statistical purposes, the Use ; and : as sentence break option counts each phrase ending with a semicolon or colon as a sentence. Press Enter if you want to enable this option. If you like to construct long sentences with colons and semicolons, you might consider enabling this option. More so than a normal sentence tabulation, it will give you a fair idea of how many "thoughts" your writing conveys.

Enable the Use slower BIOS video handling option if your video monitor displays "snow" or if it is not entirely IBM compatible.

Write errors to summary file

The Write errors to Summary file option is similar to the Generate statistics summary file option, except it generates a file containing the errors instead of the statistics. Error files have the same names as documents, but with the DOS file extension .SUM.

Exploring the Rule Classes

In this step you'll learn more about Grammatik's rule classes and how to invoke or suppress the rules in each class. You'll also learn about some of the less obvious rule classes.

WHAT IS A RULE CLASS?

English has too many rules to display individually on the user interface of a grammar-checking program. However, in order to give you more control over the rules and when you want them applied, Grammatik has grouped its rules into classes. There are 42 rule classes in Grammatik IV Version 2.0. In Version 1.0, single-word spelling is considered a rule class, bringing the total to 43. (In Version 2.0, spell-checking is a separate option on the Preferences menu.)

To see a list of the rule classes and tell which ones are currently active, select the Rule classes option on the Preferences menu of the Opening screen. You will see the submenu shown in Figure 11.1.

STEP 11

- *Figure 11.1: The Rule classes submenu*

Rule classes are divided into groups

As you can see from this submenu, the rule classes are divided into four basic groups: Grammatical, Mechanical, Style, and User-defined. In Grammatik IV Version 2.0, there is an All of the above option that lists all 42 rule classes on the Grammatical, Mechanical, and Style rule class lists. Each of the larger groups is described in this step. First, let's examine a sample rule class and learn how to turn it on or off from the Opening screen.

For our example, let's suppose we were writing dialogue in a story, and one character was always being interrupted in mid-sentence. We want to prevent Grammatik from flagging each of these sentence fragments as an incomplete sentence. To turn off the Incomplete sentence rule class, follow these steps:

1. Press P or click on Preferences with the mouse to select the Preferences menu.

2. Use the mouse or the ↓ to move the cursor to the Rule classes option, and press Enter or click the left mouse button to select it. The Rule classes submenu appears.

3. Press Enter to select Grammatical. You will see the Grammatical rule classes list, as shown in Figure 11.2. Notice the asterisk to the left of the Adverb option. It tells you that this rule class is currently selected.

4. Use the mouse or ↓ to move the asterisk down to the Incomplete sentence rule class. The *X* inside the brackets means the option is enabled.

5. Press Enter to disable the option. The *X* disappears. (At this point, you could move through the list and change any other rule classes in the Grammatical rule class list as well.)

6. Press F10 to accept the changes you have made, or Esc to abandon the changes.

Grammatical Rule Classes

The rule classes on the Grammatical list have to do with parts of speech, a part of speech being the role that a word plays in a given

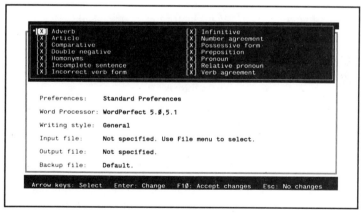

- *Figure 11.2: The Grammatical rule classes list*

STEP 11

sentence. In the sentence "I see clear now" the word *see* is a part of speech known as a verb. Because clear modifies the verb, it should correctly be changed to the adverb "clearly." Grammatik would detect this error from the Adverb rule class. It is beyond the scope of this book to describe the use and function of each rule, but what follows is a list of the Grammatical rule classes with brief samples and explanations.

Adverb	Checks for errors having to do with modifying verbs, such as the one explained above.
Article	Checks for errors having to do with articles, such as "an apples" or "a IBM computer," both of which carry the wrong article.
Comparative	Checks for comparison errors such as "as larger as," which should correctly be "as large as" or "larger than."
Double negative	Checks for double negatives such as "I don't get no respect."
Homonyms	Checks for the misuse of like-sounding words that are spelled differently, like "a pair tree."
Incomplete sentence	Checks for sentences with no verbs or no subjects.
Incorrect verb form	Checks for incompatible verb tenses, as in the phrase "I have going."
Infinitive	Checks split-infinitive errors such as "to timidly go."
Number agreement	Checks nouns preceded by numbers to make sure the noun and number agree, as in "two house" or "one houses."

Possessive form	Checks for omissions of the apostrophe in possessive endings, such as "Daves fiancée," which should be "Dave's fiancée."
Preposition	Checks for errors in prepositions—the words "through," "between," "in," "on," etc.
Pronoun	Checks for errors having to do with words such as he, she, or them, such as "its raining," which should be "it's raining."
Relative pronoun	Checks for errors such as "you're hat," which should be "your hat."
Verb agreement	Checks for mismatches of subject and verb, such as "they says."

Mechanical Rule Classes

The rule classes on the Mechanical list have to do with capitalization, spelling, and punctuation. To see the Mechanical rule classes, select Mechanical from the Rule classes option of the Preferences menu (see Figure 11.1). The list shown in Figure 11.3 appears. The Single-word spelling option is only available in Version 1.0 of Grammatik IV. Most of the rule classes in this list are fairly self-explanatory. The less obvious ones are explained below.

Number style	Governs how numbers appear in text. For instance, the numbers 1–10 are usually written out, and sentences should not start with a number.
Punctuation	Catches errors in punctuation, such as the improper placement of commas and semicolons.

```
 [X] Capitalization              [X] Question mark
 [X] Doubled word or punctuation [X] Quotation marks
 [X] Ellipsis mark               [X] Similar spelling
 [X] End of sentence punctuation [X] Split-word spelling
 [X] Number style                [X] Unbalanced (), {}, [], or "
 [X] Punctuation

 Preferences:     Standard Preferences
 Word Processor:  WordPerfect 5.0,5.1
 Writing style:   General
 Input file:      Not specified. Use File menu to select.
 Output file:     Not specified.
 Backup file:     Default.

 Arrow keys: Select   Enter: Change   F10: Accept changes   Esc: No changes
```

- *Figure 11.3: The Mechanical rule classes list*

Unbalanced (), {}, [], or "	Checks to make sure parentheses, brackets, and quote marks come in pairs.

STYLE RULE CLASSES

The rule classes on the Style list have to do, not with grammatical rules per se, but with stylistic guidelines for better writing. To see the Style rule classes, select Style under the Rule classes option of the Preferences menu (see Figure 11.1). The list shown in Figure 11.4 appears. It is beyond the scope of this book to describe the use and function of each of these guidelines, but what follows is a list of the Style rule classes with brief explanations.

Archaic	Flags words and phrases that are no longer in standard usage, such as "ofttimes" and "in the wee hours."
Cliche	Flags overused phrases, such as "of paramount importance" and "ample opportunity."

STEP 11

```
[X] Archaic                    [X] Overstated or pretentious
[X] Cliche                     [X] Paragraph problem
[X] Commonly confused          [X] Passive voice
[X] Foreign                    [X] Questionable usage
[X] Gender specific            [X] Redundant
[X] Informal or colloquial     [X] Split infinitive
[X] Jargon                     [X] Trademark
[X] Long sentence              [X] Vague adverb
[X] Long-winded or wordy

Preferences:      Standard Preferences
Word Processor:   WordPerfect 5.0,5.1
Writing style:    General
Input file:       Not specified. Use File menu to select.
Output file:      Not specified.
Backup file:      Default.

Arrow keys: Select   Enter: Change   F10: Accept changes   Esc: No changes
```

- *Figure 11.4: The Style rule classes list*

Commonly confused	Flags words that are commonly confused with other words, such as "discrete" and "discreet." Includes a brief description of the appropriate use of each.
Foreign	Flags foreign words used when acceptable English equivalents exist, such as *cause celebre* and *fait accompli*, which are better served by "popular cause" and "done deed."
Gender specific	Flags sexist words and phrases, such as "chairman" and "maiden voyage."
Informal or colloquial	Flags slang and overly casual words and phrases, such as "hands down" or "in a jiffy."
Jargon	Flags overused or misused technical terms, such as "interface" and "time frame."
Long sentence	Flags sentences longer than the number of words specified by your currently selected writing style.

Exploring the Rule Classes 75

Long-winded or wordy	Flags words or phrases that have more concise equivalents, such as "call your attention to," which is better served by "show."
Overstated or pretentious	Flags overwrought or empty words or phrases, such as "hitherto" and "held in abeyance."
Paragraph problem	Flags paragraphs that are too long or short.
Passive voice	Flags every use of the passive voice.
Questionable usage	Flags bad habits like starting sentences with "and" or "but."
Redundant	Flags repetitive phrases.
Split infinitive	Flags instances where "to" is separated from the rest of the infinitive in a verb phrase, such as "to earnestly strive."
Trademark	Flags use of trademarked product names where a generic name is more appropriate, such as "to Xerox" instead of "to photocopy."
Vague adverb	Flags overused adverbs that usually add little meaning, such as "fairly," "quite," and "rather."

COMBINING RULE CLASSES LISTS

You can modify a list of all the rule classes if you have Version 2.0 of Grammatik IV. First, select the All of the above option on the Rule classes submenu under the Preferences menu. You will see all 42 rule classes, as shown in Figure 11.5. Next, activate or suppress the rule classes here in the same manner as you would the three lists discussed above.

STEP 11

User-Defined Rule Classes

User-defined rule classes is the final Rule classes option. Select this option and you'll see the User-defined rule classes lists, shown in Figure 11.6. Here you can enable or disable any of the up to seven

```
•[X] Adverb                           [X] Number agreement
 [X] Archaic                          [X] Number style
 [X] Article                          [X] Overstated or pretentious
 [X] Capitalization                   [X] Paragraph problem
 [X] Cliche                           [X] Passive voice
 [X] Commonly confused                [X] Possessive form
 [X] Comparative                      [X] Preposition
 [X] Double negative                  [X] Pronoun
 [X] Doubled word or punctuation      [X] Punctuation
 [X] Ellipsis mark                    [X] Question mark
 [X] End of sentence punctuation      [X] Questionable usage
 [X] Foreign                          [X] Quotation marks
 [X] Gender specific                  [X] Redundant
 [X] Homonyms                         [X] Relative pronoun
 [X] Incomplete sentence              [X] Similar spelling
 [X] Incorrect verb form              [X] Split infinitive
 [X] Infinitive                       [X] Split-word spelling
 [X] Informal or colloquial           [X] Trademark
 [X] Jargon                           [X] Unbalanced (), (), [], or "
 [X] Long sentence                    [X] Vague adverb
 [X] Long-winded or wordy             [X] Verb agreement

 Arrow keys: Select   Enter: Change   F10: Accept changes   Esc: No changes
```

- *Figure 11.5: The combined rule classes list*

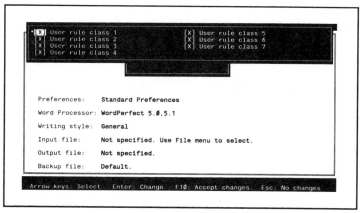

- *Figure 11.6: The User-defined rule classes list*

Exploring the Rule Classes 77

custom rule classes you can create using Grammatik's Rule and Help Editor. To learn how to create your own rules, rule classes, and rule class names using this feature, see Step 19.

Understanding the Rule Dictionaries

Grammatik groups its rules by type or class, as discussed in the previous step, and by level of strictness. Strictness groups are referred to as "rule dictionaries." In this step we will discuss differences between the rule dictionaries and how to turn them on and off.

SELECTING RULE DICTIONARIES

To see the list of rule dictionaries, select the Rule dictionaries option on the Preferences menu of the Opening screen. You'll see the Rule dictionaries list, as in Figure 12.1. Grammatik provides four dictionaries: Standard, Strict, Business, and Commonly Confused Words. Five more dictionaries are reserved for your own program customization. They are titled User Dictionary 1–4, and Inactive Rules.

How many dictionaries are active during a proofing session depends on the writing style you selected (refer to Step 9 for more details). For example, in the General writing style, all rule dictionaries are invoked except Inactive Rules.

List of active Rule dictionaries

STEP 12

```
*[X] Standard Rules              [X] User Dictionary 2
 [X] Strict Rules                [X] User Dictionary 3
 [X] Business Rules              [X] User Dictionary 4
 [X] Commonly Confused Words     [ ] Inactive Rules
 [X] User Dictionary 1


 Preferences:    Standard Preferences
 Word Processor: WordPerfect 5.0,5.1
 Writing style:  General
 Input file:     Not specified. Use File menu to select.
 Output file:    Not specified.
 Backup file:    Default.

 Arrow keys: Select   Enter: Change   F10: Accept changes   Esc: No changes
```

- *Figure 12.1: The Rule dictionaries list*

Enabling and disabling dictionaries

To turn a rule dictionary on or off, move the asterisk inside the brackets to the left of the dictionary and press Enter. Dictionaries with an *X* in the brackets next to their names are turned on; empty brackets means the dictionary is turned off. If you make any changes to the Rule dictionaries list, press F10 to accept your changes. To abandon your changes, press Esc.

THE RULE DICTIONARIES

You can speed up Grammatik's proofing function by disabling a dictionary that you don't need for your writing. The dictionaries are described below.

Standard Rules

The Standard Rules dictionary houses basic grammatical rules that you should always follow, regardless of your writing style or audience. This dictionary is turned on for all writing styles.

Strict Rules

The Strict Rules dictionary comprises stylistic rules that apply to words or phrases that are not technically incorrect, but should usually be avoided.

80 *Up & Running with Grammatik*

STEP 12

The Business Rules dictionary focuses on common weaknesses in business writing, including rigid informal expressions, jargon, and overstated or pretentious phrases. This dictionary is in effect when you use the Business writing style.

Business Rules

The Commonly Confused Words dictionary flags sets of words that are often mistaken for one another, such as "effect" and "affect," and "uninterested" and "disinterested."

Commonly Confused Words

User Dictionaries 1–4 are reserved for dictionaries you create using Grammatik's Rule and Help Editor. Creating dictionaries with this option is described in Step 19. With the Rule and Help Editor, you can make certain Grammatik rules inactive. The program keeps track of which rules you have rendered inactive and puts them in a list. Should you later decide to reactivate these rules, select the Inactive Rules option. You'll see a list of inactive rules. Place an *X* in the brackets beside the ones you want to be active again.

STEP 13

Customizing Grammatik for Your Word Processor

This step describes how to make the best use of Grammatik with your word processor. Besides learning how to make Grammatik interact more efficiently with your word processor, you'll learn about screen attributes, a feature that allows you to choose how Grammatik is displayed on your monitor. Turning the spelling feature on an off is also covered.

GETTING THE MOST FROM YOUR WORD PROCESSOR

Use Grammatik's Word processor submenu to customize Grammatik for use with your word processor. To get to the options on this submenu, select the Preferences menu on the Opening screen and select the Word processor option on the Preferences menu. Your screen will look like Figure 13.1.

You chose a word processor when you installed Grammatik on your computer. However, you'll have to choose a new one if you use more

STEP 13

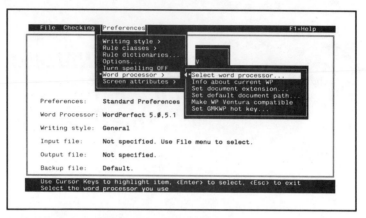

- *Figure 13.1: The Word processor submenu*

than one word processing program, have just changed to a new one, or have upgraded to a new version of your old word processing program. Fortunately, it's easy enough to change word processor selections at any time.

To change to a new word processor, choose the Select word processor option on the Word processor submenu (see Figure 13.1). You will see a list of word processors like the one displayed when you installed the program. Select a new word processor by using the mouse or arrow keys to scroll through the list and find the one you want. Next, press Enter.

If you have a mouse, you don't have to scroll through the list if you don't want to. Instead, you can see the word processors on the previous or next screen by clicking on the word More with the left mouse button. Another quick way to find your word processor on the list is to enter the first letter of its name. Grammatik will go to the first word processor beginning with the letter you entered. No matter what method you use to find your word processor, press Enter to select it.

84 *Up & Running with Grammatik*

STEP 13

If you are using one of the word processors that will work with Grammatik's hot key switch, you must have selected the correct word processor before you can run Grammatik's G4RUNWP or GMKWP program. Otherwise, Grammatik will not understand your document's file format or be able to load the appropriate word processor. The hot key switch and G4RUNWP and GMKWP program are discussed in Step 3.

Getting information about your word processor

Grammatik interacts with each word processor differently. Be sure to observe the on-screen remarks concerning yours when you install Grammatik. If you forgot to do that, you can view this information by selecting the Word processor option on the Preferences menu and then the Info about current WP option on the submenu (see Figure 13.1). You'll see a summary of the more important notes on word processors that work with the Grammatik hot key combination.

Assigning document extensions automatically

Grammatik lets you assign a DOS file name extension automatically to your documents. This is helpful when you have many files in a directory besides your documents and you only want to check documents. If you assign them all the extension .DOC, for example, you can clearly distinguish your documents from other files. To assign automatic file name extensions, select the Set document extension option on the Word processor submenu (see Figure 13.1). Next, type in an extension up to three characters long, such as TXT, and press Enter to accept your new extension as the default. If you decide to abandon the operation, press Esc.

Assigning a default document path

You can set a DOS path automatically with your documents. To assign a default document path, select the Set default document path option from the Word processor submenu (see Figure 13.1). Type in a path, which can include a drive letter followed by a colon (:), and any subdirectories followed by backslashes (\). For example, you could type

    C:\WP\DOCS

STEP 13

Paths can be up to 31 characters long. Press Enter to accept your new default path, or press Esc if you decide to abandon the operation.

Ventura-compatible processing files

Grammatik comes with a special feature for people who use their word processors to produce documents to be used with Xerox Ventura Publisher. By selecting the Make WP Ventura compatible option (see Figure 13.1), you can have Grammatik understand the desktop publishing codes that Ventura includes in documents. To turn off this feature, you must reselect your word processor with the Select word processor option.

The Set GMKWP option only applies to the most common word processing programs. Use this option to assign a specific key combination for switching to Grammatik from your word processor. If you don't specify otherwise, Grammatik uses Alt-G. For a complete list of these word processors and a full discussion of the hot key feature, review Step 3.

ASSIGNING SCREEN ATTRIBUTES

Provided you have a color monitor, you can use the Screen attributes option on the Preferences menu to establish a new color scheme for your monitor. Even if you have a monochrome monitor, you can use the Screen attributes option to choose between light text on a black background or black text on a light background. Choose the color or monochrome scheme and press Enter to see the changes. The scheme will change each time you press Enter. Play around with the color schemes until you find one you are comfortable with.

WORKING WITH GRAMMATIK SPELL-CHECKERS

Spell-checking in Version 1.0

Spelling—that is, single-word spelling—is normally turned off in Grammatik IV Version 1.0. In fact, spelling is considered a Mechanical

STEP 13

rule class. To turn spelling on, select the Rule classes option from the Preferences menu of the Opening screen. Next, select the Mechanical rule class. When the Mechanical rule class list appears on the screen, use the mouse or arrow keys to move the asterisk to the left of the Single-word spelling option. Finally, press Enter to turn on the spell-checking feature. An *X* will appear inside the brackets to indicate that the feature has been activated. To accept this change, press F10. To abandon it, press Esc.

Version 2.0 of Grammatik IV improved its spell-checker speed and ease of use. The single-word spelling checker is active by default. In Version 2.0, spell-checking is one of the main options on the Preferences menu, which makes it easier to turn spell-checking on and off. If you already checked the spelling with your word processor and want to turn spelling off, just select the Turn spelling OFF option on the Preferences menu on the Opening screen, and press Enter or click the left mouse button. The feature will be turned off, and the menu will change to read Turn spelling ON. Select it in the same manner to reactivate spelling.

Spell-checking in Version 2.0

STEP 14

Command Line Options

Grammatik IV provides you with DOS command line options, called "switches," and other shortcuts for speeding up your routine use of the program. With switches, you can access certain commands automatically when you load Grammatik into memory at the DOS command prompt. You can also instruct Grammatik to check a specific file or list of files, go directly to interactive checking, or use a specific preference file or word processor, among other things. This step describes these shortcuts and tells you how to use them.

USING COMMAND LINE SWITCHES

While Grammatik's pull-down menu design makes it easier to find commands, you may become impatient with having to pull down the same menu and select the same option over and over again. To help with this problem, Grammatik allows you to issue a common set of commands as soon as you load the program into DOS. This way, you can complete your work merely by typing a few characters. These single-letter commands issued when you load Grammatik are switches.

STEP 14

To use switches with Grammatik, you start at the DOS prompt. Type the Grammatik program you want to load (the Profiler, the Rule and Help Editor, or Grammatik itself) followed by one space, then a hyphen and the command switch. For example, to see the list shown in Figure 14.1 of DOS command switches available in Version 2.0, type

GMK -h

and press Enter. To see the list in Version 1.0, type

G4 -?

and press Enter.

You can use the -? switch with either version to bring up this list of command switches. Take a moment to look at Figure 14.1. It shows all the switches available with Grammatik.

```
[C:\GMK]gmk -?
gmk [-w] [-sw1 .. -swn] [filename]
    [allowed switches]:    -h: help.
        -b: Batch check: mark only check, exit at end.
        -g: Go. Start full checking immediately.
        -k: Keyboard only - no mouse.
        -m: Force display to Mono (black & white).
        -o out_name: copy marked output to out_name.
        -p pref_name: use pref_name.prf for preferences.
        -r: Force to coloR display.
        -w: set Word processor only.
        -x: eXplicit file names; don't use picker.
[C:\GMK]
```

- *Figure 14.1: The Command line switch help screen*

STEP 14

BATCH PROCESSING

Grammatik IV provides a feature for specifying a file to check when you load the program into memory. This allows you to skip the step of specifying an input file name once you've reached Grammatik's Opening screen. To do this, simply type

GMK *filename*

with Version 2.0, or

G4 *filename*

with Version 1.0, where *filename* is the name of the file you want checked. If you are loading Grammatik to run with your word processor, follow the same procedure, substituting GMKWP (Version 2.0) or G4RUNWP (Version 1.0) as the command before the file name. For the rest of this step we will use the Version 2.0 command in our examples.

Batch files can help you automate the checking process. For example, suppose you had a file or list of files you wanted checked. You could type

GMK -b *filename(s)*

and press Enter. Grammatik would mark all errors in the file or files you entered with the marking character. When Grammatik was done checking and marking the files, the program would close automatically and return you to the DOS prompt.

Creating a DOS Batch File

DOS batch files have the extension .BAT and they execute the DOS commands listed within them. A good example of a batch file is your AUTOEXEC.BAT file. DOS looks for it every time you turn on or reset your computer. AUTOEXEC.BAT runs each of its DOS commands

Automatic file checking

How batch files can help you

Batch files execute commands automatically

Command Line Options

STEP 14

or programs in the order given. You can create other batch files by making a file in ASCII text format with a list of DOS commands or programs, each followed by Enter, so that when you display the file each command or program appears on a separate line.

To see how batch files work, let's create a batch file to select a list of documents to check with Grammatik. At the DOS prompt, type

```
COPY CON CHECK.BAT
GMK -b file 1
GMK -b file 2
GMK -b file 3
<Ctrl-Z>
```

where *file 1, 2,* and *3* are the file names of three of your documents. Now press Enter. The first line assigns the name CHECK.BAT to the file you are about to create. You can give your batch file any DOS file name you want (it doesn't have to be CHECK.BAT) as long as it ends with the .BAT extension. When you substitute your file names for the hypothetical ones in the example, include the path if they are found on another drive or directory. Pressing F6 has the same effect as pressing Ctrl-Z, the signal for ending the batch file.

Invoking a batch file To invoke your batch file, type CHECK (or the name you chose) and press Enter at the DOS prompt.

AUTOMATIC INTERACTIVE MODE

You can specify interactive checking as a command switch. To do so, type

```
GMK -g filename
```

and press Enter.

STEP 14

You can also specify interactive mode in a batch file by substituting -g for -b, with one important distinction. You must issue the Quit command in Grammatik yourself after checking each file—you can't include the Quit command (Ctrl-C) in the batch file. When you quit Grammatik, the next line in the batch file is processed.

Batch files for interactive mode

USING GRAMMATIK WITH THE KEYBOARD ONLY

If you are using Version 2.0 of Grammatik IV, you may have reason to suppress the mouse support system. For instance, you may be without a mouse temporarily, or you may prefer using Grammatik without a mouse so as not to have the mouse pointer moving around your screen. In any case, use the -k switch (keyboard only) to disable the mouse support.

Suppressing the mouse support

MONOCHROME AND COLOR DISPLAY

If you have a color monitor but prefer to use Grammatik in monochrome, use the -m switch.

Use the -m switch to suppress color display if you have a color video card in your computer but are using a monochrome monitor. Color video cards sometimes make the Grammatik menus difficult to read onscreen.

On the other hand, if you want to specify color display at the DOS prompt, use the -r switch. Of course, you can also change these settings at any time with the Screen attributes option on the Preferences menu.

Specifying color display

Command Line Options

STEP 14

SPECIFYING AN OUTPUT FILE NAME

You can specify the name of your corrected file (the output file) as you load the program. This sometimes makes it easier to keep track of which file is the most recent draft. To give a specific output file name from the DOS command prompt, use the -o switch followed by the output file name you want. For instance, to specify the output file name LETTER.OUT, you would type

    GMK -o LETTER.OUT

and press Enter. When you see Grammatik's Opening screen, LETTER.OUT will be listed as the output file name. By including a drive letter or path, you can use this command to save the new file to a different drive or directory.

SELECTING A PREFERENCE FILE

After you've been using Grammatik for a while you will have determined which Preference file options are best for you. To select a preference file to use during your checking session from the DOS command prompt, use the -p switch followed by the name of the preference file. For instance, to specify the preference file LEGAL.PRF, you would type

    GMK -p LEGAL.PRF

and press Enter. Remember that you must specify the file extension .PRF for a preference file.

CHANGING WORD PROCESSOR SETTINGS

If you just want to change the word processor setting for Grammatik and then exit, type

    GMK -w

94 *Up & Running with Grammatik*

and press Enter at the DOS command prompt. The -w switch is particularly useful if you are using GMKWP (for Version 2.0) or G4RUNWP (for Version 1.0), because you can't change a word processor using one of these programs.

SUPPRESSING THE FILE LIST

Suppose you find you are accidentally selecting program files or other inappropriate nondocument files frequently. You may want to suppress the list of all the file names in the current directory. To do so, type

```
GMK -x
```

and press Enter at the DOS prompt. You will then need to type in the desired input file name in a dialog box. Make sure to include the drive letter and path if the input file is on another drive or directory.

Refining Spelling Dictionaries

You already know how to use Grammatik IV to check for spelling errors. While full-featured word processors all have a spell-checker of some sort, many Grammatik users find it easier to perform both grammar- and spell-checking with Grammatik. In this step you will learn how to maintain a customized version of Grammatik's dictionary, and how to delete and add words to it. Having a customized dictionary not only makes the spell-checking procedure go faster, it makes spell checks more accurate as well.

GRAMMATIK'S SPELLING DICTIONARY FILES

To check for misspelled words, Grammatik IV accesses its master spelling dictionary and compares your spellings with its own. Any word not found or not spelled the same in the dictionary is considered an error. The dictionary is kept in a file called MASTER.DIC (Master Dictionary), which is usually in the same directory as the other

How Grammatik checks for misspelled words

STEP 15

Grammatik files on your hard disk. (If you installed Grammatik to run on floppy disks alone, you may not be able to use the spelling feature.)

Adding words to the master dictionary

MASTER.DIC contains over 50,000 English words. In spite of how many words the dictionary contains, some of the words Grammatik encounters in your documents—especially product names and technical vocabulary—will not appear in the dictionary, even though they are clearly not misspelled. To remedy this situation you can have Grammatik "learn" new words—that is, you can add them to the master dictionary. Do this by pressing F7 or selecting the Learn misspelled word option (called "Learn spelling word" in Version 1.0) from the Edit menu of the Error Detection screen when Grammatik flags what it thinks is a misspelled word.

The user dictionary file

Each new word you add is stored in a file named USER.DIC (User Dictionary), which can hold about 100 words. After you've added a number of words to the user dictionary, you may see an error message stating that the user dictionary is full. This means you can no longer add words to the user dictionary until you've updated the master dictionary. When you see the error message, just press F10 to bypass the error for the time being. The next section explains how to remedy the situation by placing the words in the user dictionary in the master dictionary file.

UPDATING THE MASTER DICTIONARY

You can add the list of words that have accumulated in your USER.DIC file to the MASTER.DIC file. When you do this, the USER.DIC is emptied to make more room for new words. However, before you do this, make a backup copy of both your MASTER.DIC and USER.DIC files to either a floppy disk or another part of your hard disk. This way if you change your mind and decide to keep your original dictionary after all, you can restore it using your

98 *Up & Running with Grammatik*

STEP 15

backup copy. Grammatik does not automatically make backup copies of its dictionaries like it does your documents.

Also, be sure to have at least 200K of free disk space on your disk for the temporary files Grammatik will create when it updates the master dictionary.

To help you update the master dictionary, Grammatik provides a dictionary utility program called DICTUTIL.EXE. This program is located in the same directory as your other Grammatik files. To begin the update, log on to the Grammatik directory, type

DICTUTIL

and press Enter. You will see the screen shown in Figure 15.1.

Answer the questions as they appear onscreen. The first one asks whether or not you have a hard disk. Next the utility program will want to know what letter designation your disk drive has. (Usually you will answer C to this question.)

```
        DICTUTIL - The Reference Software Dictionary Maintenance Program
                  Version 3.30 Copyright (c) 1987-1988 Reference Software Intl.

     This program will automatically add to or delete from the master
dictionary MASTER.DIC.  The old version of the main dictionary
will be erased after it has been updated.

     Before you use this program, we suggest you make back up copies of the
current versions of MASTER.DIC and USER.DIC.  You can press Control-C to abort
operation of this program if you need to exit and make the back ups.

     If you have floppy disk drives, you will first need to prepare a
blank floppy (or use one with at least 200K of free space) to hold a temporary
working file while the dictionary is being updated.  If you don't have such
a disk, please press Control-C now and run this program again after you have
prepared the extra floppy.  Hard disk users need not use a floppy.

Does your system have a hard disk? (y/n)
```

■ *Figure 15.1: The dictionary utility*

Refining Spelling Dictionaries 99

STEP 15

Adding words

The third question asks whether you want to add words to or delete words from the master dictionary. Usually, you will want to add words to the dictionary, in which case you should type *A*. But if you are trying to squeeze Grammatik's dictionary onto a floppy disk or you added a misspelled word to the dictionary by mistake, you will want to delete words.

Deleting words

Before you can delete words from the master dictionary, you have to prepare the list of words you want deleted and store them in a file called DELETE.DIC—that is where the dictionary utility expects to find them. If you have already created the DELETE.DIC list, press *D* and Grammatik will remove the words from the master dictionary. However, if you haven't created the DELETE.DIC file you will have to abort the dictionary update procedure, create it, and start all over.

You can abort the update procedure at any time by pressing Ctrl-C.

After you've pressed *A* to tell Grammatik that you want to add words to the master dictionary, you will be asked if the new words are in the USER.DIC file. The program allows you to keep an ASCII file up to 99 words long for storing words you want to add to the master dictionary. If you've been keeping such a file, specify its name. Otherwise, the dictionary utility program will assume you want to add the new words in the USER.DIC file, and you can press *Y*.

Next, Grammatik asks if you want the USER.DIC emptied after you've updated the master dictionary. Answer *Y* if you are using the USER.DIC file to store the new words you want to add to the master dictionary. This way, you can make room for more new words. If you are updating the master dictionary with a list of your own, you can just answer *N*.

Once you've answered all the questions, you will then see the screen shown in Figure 15.2. Here you can see the master dictionary file being updated. Grammatik goes through each letter of the dictionary,

```
Reading user dictionary: C:USER.DIC
New words from user dictionary: 2
Working on letter: abcdefgh
```

- *Figure 15.2:Updating the master dictionary*

adding or deleting words. The procedure takes about a minute. You will be returned to the DOS command prompt when the update is complete.

COMMAND LINE SWITCHES TO UPDATE THE MASTER DICTIONARY

You can also use command line switches when you load the DICTUTIL.EXE utility. This makes the update procedure go faster. To use a command line switch, type

DICTUTIL -*switch*

and press Enter, where *switch* is the letter assigned to the given switch. Below is a list of command line switches with a brief description of their functions.

-?   Displays a list of available switches.

-d   Deletes words from the MASTER.DIC file.

Command line switches

Refining Spelling Dictionaries **101**

-a	Adds words to the MASTER.DIC file.
-h*d*	Specifies a hard disk drive, where *d* is the drive letter designation.
-v	Displays each word as it is being added to or deleted from the MASTER.DIC file.
-e	Empties the word list, either USER.DIC's or your own, after the update is through.
-f *filename*	Allows you to specify a file name other than USER.DIC for word strings you want to add to the master dictionary.

OTHER DICTIONARIES

Grammatik's dictionary is compatible with Reference Software's other dictionaries: the *Random House Concise Dictionary*, as well as a legal, medical, oil industry, and British dictionary. Foreign dictionaries are available as well. See the *User Guide* or contact Reference Software directly for more details about other dictionaries you can use with Grammatik.

How Grammatik Checks for Errors

The remaining steps in this book deal with advanced topics in Grammatik. Therefore, at this point it would be useful for you to know the mechanics of how Grammatik IV analyzes your documents. Once you understand the program's inner workings, you will have the insights to create your own rules, dictionaries, and help screens. This step describes the order in which each type of checking technique is applied to your document, and how Grammatik treats headings, titles, and lists.

THE ERROR CHECKING PROCESS

Grammatik analyzes your documents in a fairly straightforward way. First, the words are compared to the words in Grammatik's master dictionary—that is to the words in the MASTER.DIC file. Each word must be spelled correctly, otherwise Grammatik won't be able to identify it.

Checked by the master dictionary

Once Grammatik has identified all the words, each is assigned an appropriate part of speech. Parts of speech are the parts each type of

Assigned parts of speech

103

STEP 16

Assigning parts of speech

word plays in a sentence. In "the lazy dog slept soundly", the word "the" is an article, "lazy" an adjective, "dog" a noun, "slept" a verb, and "soundly" an adverb. Grammatik makes these assignments in order to identify certain types of grammatical errors. To see what parts of speech Grammatik has assigned to each word in your document, press F4 on the Error Detection screen.

Checked by the rule dictionaries

After it has assigned parts of speech, Grammatik compares your documents to its rule dictionaries. Rule dictionaries are lists of words and expressions known to be confusing, such as the homonyms "bear" and "bare." Rule dictionaries also contain words and phrases that are problematical, such as toward (in America) and towards (in Britain). Problematical words and phrases are identified and will be flagged when you check the file.

Checked for grammatical errors

The next step Grammatik takes is to check for grammatical errors such as verb disagreement or improper verb tense. The makers of Grammatik have created formula-like definitions for correct grammar usage. In this way, grammatical errors can be identified.

Checked for mechanical errors

Next Grammatik checks for mechanical errors. Examples of mechanical errors include misspellings, for which Grammatik can suggest replacements, incorrect or missing punctuation, and capitalization problems.

Finally, Grammatik generates the statistical summaries you see when you finish an interactive check or select the Statistics only option on the Opening screen.

ANALYZING SPECIAL TEXT

Most writing is composed of running text broken into paragraphs, with each paragraph separated from the next by a "hard carriage return." You create a hard carriage return in your word processor when you press Enter instead of letting the sentence wrap to the next line. A sentence that wraps around to the next line automatically is called a "soft carriage return." Grammatik distinguishes between hard and soft carriage returns—and for an important reason, as you will see shortly.

Many documents contain headings, titles, and lists. Of course, these are not complete sentences, and it would be annoying, for example, if each heading in your document was flagged because Grammatik thought it was an incomplete sentence. Consequently, Grammatik can tell when it has encountered a heading or title. When it finds a string of words followed, not by a punctuation mark, but by a hard carriage return and a complete sentence, it knows it has encountered a heading or title. Headings and titles are not checked for punctuation, so neither can they be flagged for being incomplete sentences.

Headings and titles

Sometimes punctuation is included in headings, however, and if you want your headings checked for punctuation, choose the Count headings in analysis option under the Options command on the Preferences menu.

Grammatik cannot recognize or analyze most lists. It can, however, recognize an item in a list if it begins with a number and is followed by one the following characters:

Lists

.)] } –

The program can also recognize and analyze phrases beginning with one of the following characters:

– * = + >

How Grammatik Checks for Errors **105**

Customizing Grammatik's Rules

You already know how Grammatik's design takes into account your individual needs by providing you with ample customization techniques. This step introduces a utility program called the Rule and Help Editor for changing the rules and help features of Grammatik. The rules are contained in a file called G4.DIC (in Version 1.0) or GMK.DIC (in Version 2.0). This step, which includes a sample exercise, shows you how to edit existing rules contained in this file.

THE RULE AND HELP EDITOR

To start the Rule and Help Editor in Version 1.0, go to the DOS prompt, type

G4RHED

and press Enter. In Version 2.0, type

GMKED

and press Enter.

STEP 17

File menu options

Besides the Help menu, the Rule and Help Editor offers two other menus, File and Edit. Let's look at the File menu first. Select it by typing *F* or by clicking on the File menu. You will see the following options:

- Quit—save work (Q);
- Cancel—no changes;
- Merge ASCII rules;
- Write user rules to ASCII file; and
- About the Rule and Help Editor.

Quit, Cancel, and the last option, About the Rule and Help Editor, are self-explanatory. Quit exits the program and saves the changes you've made to Grammatik's rules. Select the Cancel—no changes option if you decide to abandon your work and keep the rules and help features intact. About the Rule and Help Editor gives you some explanatory information about the function of this utility program.

Use the merge ASCII rules and Write user rules to ASCII file options to preserve your customizing efforts when you upgrade your copy of Grammatik to a newer version. If you put a lot of work into formulating new and modified rules, you will want to have a copy of that work. That way you can transfer the custom rules to your new copy of Grammatik's rule dictionary (GMK.DIC or G4.DIC).

Transferring customized rules

To transfer customized rules to a newer version of Grammatik, start in the old version and select the Write user rules to ASCII file option. Now that your customized rules are on-disk, go ahead and install the newer version of the program. Next, from the newer version, select the Merge ASCII rules option and specify where the file you saved with the old version is. Grammatik will transfer the old rules to the new rule dictionary.

You can also use the Merge ASCII rules option to merge a list of new rules into your rule dictionary. To do this, your rules must be stored in ASCII file format. See Grammatik's *User's Guide* for more details on this feature.

Let's look at the Edit menu now. You can reach it by pressing *E* or clicking on Edit from the Opening screen of the Rule and Help Editor. The Edit menu options are described below:

Edit menu options

Rules (R)	allows you to edit or suppress existing rules and add or delete rules of your own making.
Rule class names (C)	allows you to assign a name to the rule classes you create.
Dictionary names (D)	allows you to assign a name to the rule dictionaries you create.
Count category names	allows you to assign a name to the rule count categories you create.
Help entries (H)	allows you to modify the text of existing help screens to suit your own needs.

In this step we will primarily concern ourselves with the first Edit menu option, Rules.

MODIFYING RULES

Let's modify an existing rule to give you an idea how the Rule and Help Editor can make your copy of Grammatik more useful. The rule we will modify has to do with sexist language. Specifically, we will find Grammatik's rule about not using the term "horsemanship," and we will add a better term to use in its place—"equestrian skill"—in the rule's advice section.

Changing an existing rule

Before we begin, make sure you are in the directory containing Grammatik's program files. Make sure as well that you're in the Rule

STEP 17

and Help Editor. If you're not and you have Version 2, type

GMKED

at the DOS prompt and press Enter. In Version 1.0, type

G4RHED

and press Enter. Now, in the Rule and Help editor,

The Rules screen

1. Press **E** to select the Edit menu on the Opening screen.
2. Press **R** to select the Rules option on the Edit menu.

You will see the Rules screen, which is shown in Figure 17.1. On this screen you can view the rules and accompanying advice from Grammatik's rule dictionary. Take a moment to scroll down this screen and look at some of the rules. Each rule, in effect, is a hard and fast lesson in good writing. The Rules screen has three menus—Select Rules, Change Rule, and, on the right side, Help.

3. Press **S** to choose the Select rule option. You will see the Select Rules menu in Figure 17.2.

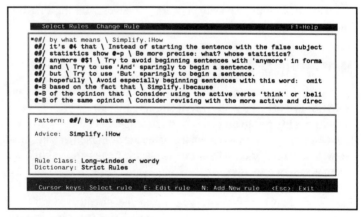

- *Figure 17.1: The rules screen*

110 *Up & Running with Grammatik*

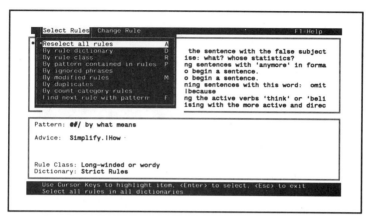

- *Figure 17.2: The Select Rules menu*

The Select Rules menu allows you to search for the rule you wish to change or modify. Notice how the rule categories are arranged by sorting criteria. We are looking for the word "horsemanship," so we need to look for a rule by searching for a specific pattern of characters—"man." That means we'll select the fourth option down, By pattern contained in rules.

The Select Rules menu

Before we do that, though, remember that each time you select a sorting criteria on the Select Rule menu, you effectively narrow the set of rules that Grammatik displays. To see all the rules again, choose the first option, Reselect all rules (A).

4. Press **P** to activate the By pattern contained in rules option. You will see the Pattern dialog box shown in Figure 17.3.

The Pattern dialog box is where you tell Grammatik which word to bring up. Here we can either enter the word "horsemanship" directly or we can enter the asterisk (*) wildcard character and the letters "man." With the second method, Grammatik will search for all combinations of letters that include the syllable "man."

The Pattern dialog box

Customizing Grammatik's Rules **111**

STEP 17

```
 Select Rules  Change Rule                               F1=Help
*@#/ by what means \ Simplify.|How
 @#/ it's @4 that \ Instead of starting the sentence with the false subject
 @#/ statistics show @-p \ Be more precise: what? whose statistics?
 @#/ anymore @$1 \ Try to avoid beginning sentences with 'anymore' in forma
 @#/ and \ Try to use 'And' sparingly to begin a sentence.
 @#/ but \ Try to use 'But' sparingly to begin a sentence.
 @#/ hopefully \ Avoid especially beginning sentences with this word:  omit
              Select by Pattern Contained in Rule
 Enter pattern? *man

 Pattern: @#/ by what means
 Advice:  Simplify.|How


 Rule Class: Long-winded or wordy
 Dictionary: Strict Rules
     Use Cursor Keys to highlight item, <Enter> to select, <Esc> to exit
     Select rules by a pattern contained in the rule
```

- *Figure 17.3: The Pattern dialog box*

The Pattern dialog box also lets you look for a noun and its plural forms. In this case, you would type in a combination of letters followed by the underscore (_) wildcard character. Grammatik would search for the combination of letters you entered followed by *s* or *es*. Let's use the asterisk wildcard character and bring up all sexist words with the syllable "man."

5. Type

   *man

   and press Enter. After a few seconds, you will see the screen shown in Figure 17.4.

This screen lists sexist words with the syllable "man" and rules for their correct usage. The rule highlighted in Figure 17.4 warns you not to use the gender-specific words "horsemanship" and "horsewomanship".

We want to add the term "equestrian skill" to the advice selection of the word "horsemanship." With "horsemanship" highlighted,

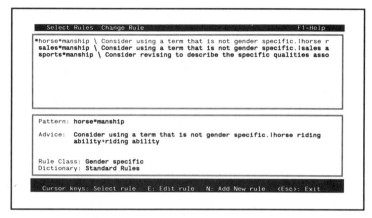

- *Figure 17.4: Displaying rules with a given pattern*

    6. Press **E** to edit the current rule. You will see the dialog box in Figure 17.5.

Notice the message in the center of the screen prompting you to select an item to edit. At present the Pattern item is highlighted. For our purposes, we will leave the rule pattern alone, and add only to the advice section.

    7. Press ↓ once to highlight Advice.

Notice now the vertical bar character (¦) marks the end of the rule statement and the beginning of suggested replacement words. These are the same replacement words or phrases you see when you press F2 (and F3 as well in Version 2.0) during an interactive proofing session. Notice that the two phrases given are separated by an arrow pointing right. Let's add our possible replacement to this list.

    8. With Advice highlighted, press **Enter**. Now the text of the advice is displayed in a dialog box above the rule.

    9. Use the cursor keys or mouse to move the cursor to the end of the advice.

Customizing Grammatik's Rules **113**

STEP 17

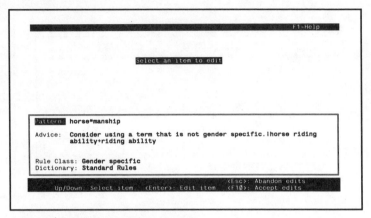

- *Figure 17.5: Selecting an item to edit*

   10. Press the **Tab** key. You will see a new arrow pointing right. This separates the last replacement phrase from the new one you're about to enter.

   11. Type

   equestrian skill

   12. Press **F10** twice to accept the Advice edit and exit from the Edit selected rule option.

   13. Press **Esc** to exit the Rules menu and type **Y** to confirm the edit.

   14. Press **Q** to exit the Rule and Help Editor.

The next time Grammatik flags the word "horsemanship" in your document, you'll have a third term to use as a replacement—"equestrian skill." In this way you can compile a thesaurus of customized terms to improve your writing.

Making Your Own Rules

The last step introduced you to the Rule and Help Editor and showed you how to perform a simple modification to an existing rule. In this step, you will learn how to create a simple new rule, include some advice to display on the screen when it is invoked, and assign it to a rule class. Assigning a new rule to a class is very important for incorporating the rule into existing writing style and preference file specifications. Finally, you will see the rule in action.

ADDING NEW RULES

Grammatik comes with a set of programming functions so you can represent—or invent—very sophisticated rules of your own. The programming functions are briefly described in the next step. At this point we will use a very simple example to create a new rule. This way you can see how the process works.

A pattern is the simplest rule you can define with Grammatik. When you define a specific pattern of letters, you tell Grammatik to stop when it encounters the pattern and give you a warning. This way, you

Pattern rules

STEP 18

can edit the text or enter replacement words or phrases. For this example exercise, suppose you know a Gothic romance writer who loves obscure terms. This writer overuses the word "tessellated." To help him, you will write a rule to warn him when he uses the word. Your rule will offer a couple of familiar terms as replacements.

Before you start making the rule, make sure you are in the directory containing Grammatik's program files. Be sure as well that you've started the Rule and Help Editor by typing GMKED (Version 2.0) or G4RHED (Version 1.0) at the DOS prompt, as described in Step 17. Then follow these steps:

1. Type **R** to select the Edit Rules option.

2. Press **C** to activate the Change Rule menu, as shown in Figure 18.1. (You can bypass the Change Rule Menu and begin making a new rule immediately by pressing *N*, Add New Rule.)

The Change Rule menu

Notice on the Change Rule menu that you can also make Grammatik's built-in rules inactive, remove rules, or restore removed rules. You might consider using one of these options later on.

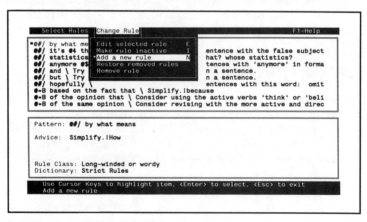

- *Figure 18.1: Adding a new rule*

116 *Up & Running with Grammatik*

3. Press **N** to add a new rule. Notice that "Pattern" is highlighted.
4. Press **Enter** to move the cursor to the Pattern section of the new rule.
5. Type

    tessellated

    Now your screen should like Figure 18.2.
6. Press **F10** to accept the edit.
7. Press **Enter** to edit the advice.
8. Type the following advice:

    There you go using 'tessellated' again. What's with you? Consider replacement.
9. Press the **vertical bar** (¦) to signify that replacements are to follow.

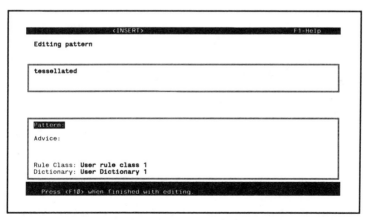

- *Figure 18.2: The Add rule screen*

STEP 18

10. Type

    checkered

    and press **Tab**. A right arrow (→) will appear when you do.

11. Type

    mosaic

    and press **F10** to tell Grammatik that you've finished editing the advice.

INTEGRATING NEW RULES INTO THE WRITING STYLE SYSTEM

Rule Class and Dictionary designation

At the bottom of the Add rule screen is the Rule Class and Dictionary designation (see Figure 18.2). The Rule Class designation is "User rule class 1," and the Dictionary designation is "User Dictionary 1." As you learned earlier, all rule classes and dictionaries are not active all the time. You must assign each new rule to an existing rule class—if there is an appropriate one—or to a user rule class that you have established for the styles you will be using. This way, your new rule will fit into Grammatik's writing style system.

Likewise, you select a rule dictionary based on how strict you think your new rule is and how often you want it to be activated. In the next part of the exercise you will assign the new rule to one of the existing rule classes.

1. Press **Enter**. You will see a list of existing rule classes.

2. Use the cursor keys or mouse pointer to scroll down the list until you reach "Overstated or pretentious," as shown in Figure 18.3.

3. Press **Enter** to select this rule class.

4. At this point you could also change the dictionary in an analogous manner, by selecting from the list of existing

dictionaries. Let's leave this option alone though and press **F10** to accept the edits. You'll see the new rule in the list, as shown in Figure 18.4.

5. Press **Esc** to exit from the Rules menu.
6. Press **Q** to exit the Rule and Help Editor.

- *Figure 18.3: Setting the rule class*

- *Figure 18.4: The new rule as it appears in the list*

STEP 18

To test out the new rule, create a file containing the word "tessellated" in your word processor. When you perform an interactive check on the file, Grammatik will flag your "tessellated" error.

Defining Complex Rule Patterns

In the last step, you learned how to create a simple rule for finding a specific pattern of characters. You also learned how to include advice for avoiding the word, and how to enter replacement words or phrases. Using more advanced techniques, you can define quite complex patterns. While it is beyond the scope of this book to explain all the possibilities, this step describes the construction set for building complex rules. It also offers a few examples.

PARTS OF A RULE PATTERN

Rule patterns are composed of what Grammatik refers to as "tokens." A token can be a word, a wildcard, or a "parsing rule" (parsing rules are explained shortly). Because Grammatik must observe certain size constraints, each rule

Rule size limitations

- can comprise 16 tokens at most;
- can contain no more than 125 characters; and

STEP 19

- cannot exceed 250 total characters, including those in the rule pattern and advice statement.

In addition, the first character of a rule pattern must be a letter of the alphabet, not a number or symbol.

Word tokens In Step 18 you defined a one-word rule pattern. Each word used in defining a rule counts as one token.

Wildcard tokens Another type of rule-pattern token is the wildcard. The asterisk (*) is the wildcard token you'll use most often. It functions the same way it does in DOS commands: you use it as a placeholder to indicate that any character or number of characters may appear in its location. For example, if you wanted to find all occurrences of "salesman," "salesmen," "saleswoman," and "saleswomen," you would define the pattern as

```
sales*n
```

The underscore character (_) is the other rule-pattern wildcard used by Grammatik. It is used solely to look for plural forms. That is, it searches for a pattern ending in *s* or *es*. For example, if you wanted to find the word "hound" as well as its plural form "hounds," you would define the pattern as

```
hound_
```

Parsing rule tokens The last type of token is the parsing rule. "To parse" a sentence means to assign each of its words a part of speech. A parsing rule gives Grammatik instructions on how to understand word patterns and parts of speech.

HOW PARSING RULES ARE FORMULATED

There are three parts to a parsing rule. First, each parsing rule begins with an at sign (@). Next comes one or more operators to tell

Grammatik how to carry out a logical operation. Finally, the parsing rule must include a part or parts of speech.

To see how parsing rules work, let's consider a practical example. Suppose you tend to overuse the verb "finesse" and you want to try to avoid doing so by establishing a new rule. You couldn't simply look for the pattern "finesse" and then establish the rule, because "finesse" is a noun as well as a verb, and you're only interested in its verb form. To find all instances of the verb "finesse," you would start from the Rule and Help Editor by typing GMKED (Version 2.0) or G4RHED (Version 1.0) at the DOS prompt. Next, you would select Rules from the Edit menu, and the select Add a new rule (N) option from the Change rule menu. Then you would press Enter and type

```
finess* @|GRTV
```

Let's look at this rule one part at a time.

The pattern "finess*"—with the asterisk wildcard—covers all verb endings, including "he finessed it," "I'll finesse it," and "she finesses it."

Next comes the at sign (@) to indicate that a parsing rule is coming.

The vertical bar (|) is the operator. It tells Grammatik that the rule is defined as any pattern intersecting with the parts of speech that follow the operator—in this case GRTV.

GRTV are the codes for present participle (G), past participle (R), past tense (T), and infinitive forms of the verb (V), respectively. A list of these codes follows later in this step.

So, the rule means "Find any word beginning with the letters *finess* if the word is one of the following parts of speech: present participle, past participle, past tense, or verb infinitive." Once you've defined the parsing rule, you could add some advice and replacement words for avoiding the verb "finesse."

RULE PATTERN OPERATORS

Below is a list of operators and an explanation of their use.

!   The Not operator is used as a negative. When it precedes another operator, it has the effect of negating it. Example:

    `!=`

means "not equal to."

<   The Shift Next operator is placed before a second operator to make the second one affect the token one token left of the one it normally would. The Shift Next operator is useful because rules must begin with an alphabetical character. Therefore, when you want to reverse the programming syntax of a rule in order to make it start with a word, you can use the Shift Next operator. Example:

    `know @< in the`

matches the pattern "in the know."

The Shift Next operator can also be used in conjunction with the Set Shift Count operator (+) and a number to make the operation apply to a token a specific number of places to the left of the operator. Example:

    `bind @<+5 caught`

finds the expression "caught in a bind."

¦   The Intersect operator is used with a part of speech to tell Grammatik that the pattern that follows can match one or more of the parts of speech assigned to it. Example:

green @¦NA

finds "green" either as a noun (N) or an adjective (A).

~ The Not Intersect operator is used with a part of speech to tell Grammatik that the pattern and part of speech cannot match one or more of the parts of speech assigned to it. Example:

green @~N

finds "green" only when it is not a noun.

^ The Subset operator is used with a part of speech to tell Grammatik that the pattern must be a subset of the parts of speech assigned to it. Example:

@^GRTV

means the word must either be a present participle, past participle, past tense, or infinitive of a verb.

= The Equals operator is used with a part of speech to tell Grammatik that the pattern must match the part of speech assigned to it. Example:

dresses @=s

matches "dresses" only when it is a plural noun.

+ The Set Shift Count operator is used in conjunction with the Shift operator (<) and a number from 0 to 9 to move the action of the parsing rule to a token 0 to 9 places to the left of it in the rule pattern.

\> The Match Next operator is used in conjunction with the Shift Next operator (<) to find words only when they occur together. Example:

one and only @+4 @<> the

Defining Complex Rule Patterns **125**

finds occurrences of "the one and only." You could do this by typing the phrase "the one and only," but then Grammatik would stop at every occurrence of "the" in your document, slowing down the checking process considerably. This way, you can search for the least common word in a phrase of several words and keep the program running efficiently.

\#   The Position operator tells Grammatik that a sentence position parsing rule follows. Use this operator to identify a word only when it comes at the beginning or end of a sentence. To signify the beginning, follow it with a slash (/); to signify the end of a sentence, follow it with a period (.). Example:

       `@#/ but`

finds sentences starting with "but." Notice that this beginning of sentence specification is an exception to the rule that all rule patterns must begin with an alphabetical pattern. If you are creating your rules in an ASCII file, you must begin with "but" instead.

0–9   The numerals 0 through 9 following the at sign (@) are used as "Span Count" operators. Span Count operators allow you to specify a number of words that may separate elements you are describing in your expression. This is useful because many expressions are separated by other words when used in an actual sentence. Example:

       `giv* @4 the evil eye`

finds most constructions of the expression, "to give the evil eye," including "he gives the stranger the evil eye" and "that woman always gives him the evil eye."

\$ The Set Match Count operator is used with a number from 1 to 9 to help with replacement words. When you are matching a pattern, Grammatik keeps track of how many words match, so that you can put the replacement word in the right position. However, this number can be higher than the actual number of words in your document if you are using shift or count operators. The Set Match Count operator allows you to set the number of matched words.

PARSING CODES FOR PARTS OF SPEECH

Below is a list of parsing codes for the parts of speech. These are used in conjunction with the rule pattern operators in order to further define rule patterns.

a	article
A	adjective
B	the verb "to be"
c	conjunction
d	adverb
G	present participle
I	"to" in a verb infinitive
M	modal
N	singular noun
p	pronoun
P	preposition
R	past participle
s	plural noun
T	past tense of a verb

Defining Complex Rule Patterns

STEP 19

V	base or infinitive of a verb
'	possessive pronoun
#	number
,	punctuation mark

Where Do You Go from Here?

Throughout this book we've touched on the major features of Grammatik and explained how the program works. In this step, we'll describe how Grammatik can help bring your writing to its fullest potential. At the end of this step is a list of resources to help you become a more effective writer.

BUSINESS WRITING AND CORPORATE PUBLISHING

The business community puts out a tremendous amount of writing—everything from brief business letters, to corporate reports, to book-length publications such as product manuals. When business people present themselves to clients and customers, they want to appear articulate, knowledgeable, and reliable. Writing samples that are clear, direct, and free of errors make an excellent first impression.

In all but the largest corporations, however, no one oversees the quality of the writing. Most businesses don't have an editorial staff

STEP 20

of editors and proofreaders. Of course, Grammatik can't do the work of a real editor—trust me and my editor on this. It can, however, be an excellent tool for improving writing quality. Grammatik takes care of the mechanics of writing—syntax, spelling, and punctuation—quite nicely.

Unless your company serves out-of-the-ordinary clients, you should select the Business writing style for your work, because business writing tends to be on the formal side, and almost all of the rules are turned on in the Business writing style.

Choose rule classes to suit your specific needs

Review the Style rule class closely. Look at the rule classes in light of your company's unique aspects, and decide which rule classes suit you best. For instance, if you produced mail-order wedding stationery, you would likely suppress the Cliche rule class, because your more traditional customers would prefer the tried and true expressions of sentiment. Or if you ran a luxury-car dealership, you would likely want to give the air of dignity to your correspondence. This would mean turning off the Overstated or pretentious rule class. If you ran a small mechanical engineering or software company, you would find the Business style less appropriate than the Technical one for your correspondence and writing about technical matters.

Developing a "house style"

Publishing houses all have what is called a "house style." For example, at Sybex, the publisher of this book, it is the house style to capitalize all DOS commands and abbreviate the word "megabyte" with the letters Mb. House styles are designed to give books consistency—and therefore legitimacy. A corporate house style would be a set of style guidelines to help writers present a consistent tone throughout all the writing they do for the company. To this end you could add your product names to the spelling dictionary, or make them into rules. This way, someone using the incorrect term in promotional literature would be reminded of the proper term and offered a replacement word.

Even experienced writers overuse certain words, phrases, or sentence constructions. These are usually referred to as "writers' tics." With the aid of the Rule and Help Editor, you can set count categories and create new style rules to keep track of tics. In this way you can avoid them.

FICTION WRITING

Fiction writing is the most varied in style. Many of the stricter rules are disabled in the Fiction style to give you more freedom in your prose. Depending on your individual style, you may want to keep these rules active. Look through the Options list and Rule class option (particularly the Style rule class) on the Preferences menu to see if you want to change anything. Then save your customized settings in a preferences file. You could have several different preference files for different types of fiction writing.

ADVERTISING COPYWRITING

Advertising copywriters and marketing staff can use Grammatik to monitor the structure of their ads and meet target criteria. For instance, you can make sure product names are mentioned with a certain degree of frequency. Or, you can simply make sure that the correct product names are being used. To this end you can use the Word Usage option with the Profiler, or Count categories.

One of the cardinal rules of advertising copywriting is to use short and punchy sentences. You might consider lowering the permissible long sentence length from the standard 30 words down to 15 words.

Gauge your copy's reading level with the statistical summary at the end of a document check. In this way you can ensure that it is appropriate for your target audience.

STEP 20

If you wanted to be especially lively, you could even use the statistical summary to make sure there are enough exclamation points in copy.

BECOMING A BETTER READER

Besides practice, one of the best ways to improve your writing is to become a conscious and more careful reader. When you come across a piece of writing that is especially effective or moving, stop and ask yourself how the writer achieved his or her effects. Study the imagery the writer used and ask yourself what makes it so compelling. Look at the length of the sentences and the degree of word complexity. Good writing has a steady and even rhythm. Study the writer's use of punctuation to see how he or she was able to tie thoughts together and build to a convincing conclusion.

ADDITIONAL RESOURCES

Below is a list of high-quality style guides and reference works to help you to become a better writer. The book provided with Grammatik IV, *Secrets of Successful Writing* by Dewitt H. Scott, also provides practical writing tips for improving your writing with Grammatik.

For further reading ...

- Flesch, Randolph. *Say What You Mean.* Harper & Row, 1972. A guide to what the author calls "open-shirt and blue-jeans writing" for business people. Includes specific instruction in the principles of professional writing and a blacklist of sixty words to avoid.

- Graves, Robert and Alan Hodge. *The Reader Over Your Shoulder: A Handbook for Writers of English Prose.* Random House, 1979. This comprehensive book by the author of *I, Claudius* is an excellent reference for fiction writers and others interested in how to write elegant and moving prose. Includes the authors' twenty-five principles for grace of expression, as well as a detailed examination of passages by Hemingway, D.H. Lawrence, and others.

- Orwell, George. "Politics and the English Language" in *The Orwell Reader.* Harcourt, Brace and Company, 1956. Besides a lively discussion of what the author considers the moral degeneracy of modern English, this essay by the author of *1984* and *Animal Farm* offers techniques for avoiding pretentious diction, meaningless words, and dying metaphors.

- Strunk, William, Jr. and E.B. White. *The Elements of Style.* MacMillan, 1979. This slender classic is required reading in most college composition courses. The authors discuss principles of composition, commonly misused words and expressions, and the basics of spelling and punctuation. Includes twenty-one rules for writing clearly and succinctly, as well as the authors' famous advice to "Omit needless words!"

- Zinsser, William. *On Writing Well: An Informal Guide to Writing Nonfiction.* Harper & Row, 1988. An entertaining, easy-to-follow guide by the former Life Magazine columnist. Explains how to organize letters, articles, and other writing for maximum clarity and understanding.

Index

A

adding rules, 115–120
adverbs, rule classes for, 72, 76
advertising copywriting, 131–132
advice, 27–28
  in documents, 29–30
  on Error Detection window, 35
  option for, 66
  removing, 30–31
alphabetical word list sort, 55
archaic words, rule class for, 74
arrow keys, 10, 37
articles, rule class for, 72
ASCII rules, merging, 108–109
asterisks (*) as wildcard, 111, 122
at sign (@) with parsing, 122–123
attributes, screen, 86
AUTOEXEC.BAT file, 4, 91
automatic interactive mode, 92–93

B

Backspace key, 37
backup files
  extensions for, 22–23
  for program disks, 1–3

batch processing, 91–93
Business writing, 129–131
  rules dictionary for, 81
  style for, 58–59

C

carets (^) as operator, 125
carriage returns, 104–105
Change Rule menu, 116
Checking menu, 11–12
cliches, rule class for, 74
colloquial words, rule class for, 75
colons (:), option for, 68
color monitors
  attributes for, 86
  specifying, 93
command line switches, 89–95, 101–102
comments, advice, 30
commonly confused words
  dictionary for, 81
  rule class for, 75
comparatives, rule class for, 72
comparison charts, 52–54
complexity statistics, 43–47
context-sensitive help, 12
corporate publishing, 129–131
count categories, 55
customizing
  comparison charts, 53–54

options for, 63–68
with Preferences menu, 12, 23–25, 63
rules, 107–114
and word processors, 83–86
writing styles, 60–62

D

Del key, 37
DELETE.DIC file, 100
dialog boxes, 11
dictionaries
  rule, 79–81, 104, 109
  spelling, 40, 97–103
DICTUTIL.EXE program, 99, 101
directories, 3–4
dollar sign ($) as operator, 126–127
DOS file names, option for, 67
double negatives, rule class for, 72

E

Edit menus, 109
editing
  errors, 35–40
  full interactive checking mode for, 33–34
  rules, 109–114
Editing window, 34–35
ellipses (...), 11

End key, 38
Equals operator (=), 125
Error Detection screen, 27–28, 30, 34–35
errors
  bypassing, 40–41
  checking for, 103–105
  correcting, 35–40
  marking, 28–29, 39–40
  printing, 67
  saving, 68
exclamation points (!)
  option for, 65
  as parsing operator, 124
  statistics for, 51
extensions, 22–23, 85
extracting programs, 7–8

F

Fiction writing, 59, 131
file lists, suppressing, 95
File menu, 11, 108–109
files, selecting, 21–25
Flesch-Kincaid Grade Level index, 50, 53
Flesch Reading Ease score, 50, 53
floppy disks
  backup copies on, 1–3
  installation onto, 5–7
foreign words
  options for, 66–67
  rule class for, 75

frequency word list sort, 55
full interactive checking mode, 27, 33–34
function keys, 35–36

G

.GB4 extension, 22
.GBK extension, 22
gender specific rule class, 58, 75, 112–114
General writing style, 58
GMK directory, 3
Grade level index averages, 45, 50–51, 53
grammatical errors
  ignoring, 41
  option for, 66
  proofing for, 27–30, 104
  rule classes for, 71–73
greater than symbol (>)
  as parsing operator, 125–126
  for submenus, 11
Gunning's Fog Index, 50–51

H

hard carriage returns, 104–105
hard disks, installation onto, 3–5
headings, options for, 65, 105
Help menu, 12
Hemingway, Ernest, comparison charts for, 52–53
Home key, 38
homonyms, rule class for, 72
hot keys, 17–19, 21, 85
house styles, 130

I

Inactive Rules dictionary, 81
incomplete sentences
  option for, 65
  rule class for, 72
incorrect verb forms, rule class for, 72
infinitives, rule class for, 72
informal words, rule class for, 75
Informal writing style, 59
input files, selecting, 21–22
Ins key, 37–38
Insert mode, 36–37
INSTALL file, 3
installation
  manual, 7–8
  onto floppy disks, 5–7
  onto hard disks, 3–5
interactive mode
  automatic, 92–93
  full, 27, 33–34
Intersect operator (I), 123–125

J

jargon, rule class for, 75

L

Learn misspelled word option, 40, 98
less than sign (<) as operator, 124
life insurance policy, comparison charts for, 52–53
Lincoln, Abraham, comparison charts for, 52–53
line breaks with Professional Write, 19
lists, 105
literal nouns, option for, 67
long sentences
　options for, 66–67
　rule class for, 75
　statistics for, 51–52
long-winded structures, rule class for, 76

M

manual installation, 7–8
marking character, option for, 67
marking errors, 28–29, 39–40
MASTER.DIC file, 6, 97–103
Match Next operator (>), 125–126
mechanical errors
　checking for, 104
　rule classes for, 73–74, 87
menus, selecting from, 10–11
merging ASCII rules, 108–109
monochrome monitors, 93
mouse
　disabling, 93
　support for, 10

N

names
　for backup files, 22
　for output files, 23
　for rules, 109
NOT operator (!), 124
Not Intersect operator (~), 125
notes on word processors, 5, 7, 19–20
number agreement, rule class for, 72
number style, rule class for, 73
numerals (0–9) as operators, 126

O

Opening screen, 10
operators, rule pattern, 124–127
options, modifying, 63–68
output files, selecting, 23, 94
overstated words, rule class for, 76
Overtype mode, 37

P

paragraph marks with Microsoft Word, 19

paragraphs
  length of, 47, 51, 53
  option for, 65
  rule class for, 76
parsing rules, 122–124
  codes for, 127–128
  operators for, 124–127
parts of speech
  assigning, 103–104
  parsing for, 122–124, 127–128
  for statistics, 43
  viewing, 42
passive voice
  rule class for, 76
  statistics for, 45–46, 51
paths, 4, 85–86
patterns
  for creating rules, 115–117
  for editing rules, 111–114
  operators for, 124–127
  with parsing, 123
  parts of, 121–122
periods (.)
  in DOS file names, 67
  with parsing operators, 126
PgUp and PgDn keys, 38
phrases
  bypassing, 41
  checking, 105
plural forms, wildcard character for, 122
plus sign (+) as operator, 124–125
Position operator (#), 126

possessive forms, rule class for, 73
pound signs (#)
  for marking errors, 28–29
  as parsing operator, 126
Preferences menu and files, 12, 23–25, 63, 94
prepositions
  rule class for, 73
  statistics for, 52–53
pretentious words, rule class for, 76
printing of errors, option for, 67
Professional Write, line breaks with, 19
program disks, backing up, 1–3
programming rules, 115–120
pronouns, rule class for, 73
proofing
  for grammatical and spelling errors, 27–30, 86–87, 104
  selecting files for, 21–25
  with word processors, 15–19
  for writing analysis, 30
proper nouns, option for, 65
punctuation
  option for, 65
  rule class for, 73–74

Q

question marks (?)
  with command switches, 90
  option for, 65

statistics for, 51–52
questionable usage, rule class for, 76

R

Read only option, 30
readability statistics, 43–47, 50–51, 66
Reading ease score index, 45
reading to improve writing, 132
README.TXT file, 5, 7
redundancies, rule class for, 76
relative pronouns, rule class for, 73
removing advice, 30–31
replacement words with rules, 39, 113–114, 117–118
resources for writing, 132–133
Rule and Help Editor, 107–114, 123
Rule Class and Dictionary designation, 118
rule classes
   combining, 76
   grammatical, 71–73
   mechanical, 73–74, 87
   menu for, 69–71
   for new rules, 118
   style, 74–76
   user-defined, 77–78
Rule/Help editor, 6
rules
   classes of. *See* rule classes
   creating, 115–120
   customizing, 107–114
   dictionaries for, 79–81, 104, 109
   parsing, 122–128
   patterns for. *See* patterns
   and writing styles, 58–60
Rules screen, 110

S

saving
   changes, 39
   error files, 68
   readability statistics, 66
screen attributes, 86
Select Rules menu, 111
semicolons (;), option for, 68
sentence length
   options for, 66–67
   statistics for, 45–46, 51–53
   in writing styles, 59
Set Match Count operator ($), 126–127
Set Shift Count operator (+), 124–125
Shift Next operator (<), 124
short sentences
   options for, 66–67
   statistics for, 51–52
shortcut keystrokes, 12
single-word spelling, 40–41, 58
skipping problems, 36
slashes (/) with operators, 126

soft carriage returns, 105
sorting
 rules, 111
 word lists, 55
Span Count operators (0–9), 126
special text, 104–105
spelling errors
 bypassing, 40–41
 dictionaries for, 40, 97–103
 proofing for, 27–30, 86–87
split infinitives, rule class for, 72, 76
Standard Rules dictionary, 80
starting, 9–11
statistics, 30
 for readability, 43–47, 50–51, 66
 for style, 49–52
Strict Rules dictionary, 80
Style rule classes, 41, 74–76, 130. *See also* writing style submenus, 11
Subset operator (^), 125
.SUM (summary) files, 66, 68
Summary screen, 30, 44–47
switches, command line, 89–95
syllables per word, 46–47, 51

T

Technical writing style, 59
text editing keys, 37–38
tics, 131

tilde (~) as operator, 125
titles, 105
toggle switches, 63
tokens, 121–122
tour, 12–13
trademarks, rule class for, 76
transferring customized rules, 108

U

unbalanced punctuation, rule class for, 74
underscore (_) wildcard character
 for editing rules, 112
 for rule-pattern tokens, 122
updating spelling dictionary, 98–102
user-defined rule classes, 77–78
User Dictionaries, 81
user interface, 9–13
USER.DIC file, 98–100, 102

V

vague adverbs, rule class for, 76
Ventura Publisher, codes with, 86
verb agreement, rule class for, 73
verb forms, rule class for, 72
vertical bars (|)
 as Intersect operator, 123–125
 for rule replacements, 113, 117

W

wildcard characters with rules, 111–112, 122
Word, paragraph marks with, 19
word processors
   customizing for, 83–86
   proofing with, 15–19
   selecting, 4–5, 7
   settings for, 94–95
WordPerfect
   document names with, 19
   hot keys for, 18
words
   dictionaries for, 97–103
   statistics for, 46–47, 52–53
   usage profile for, 54–55
words per sentence, 45, 51
WordStar, working with, 17, 19–20
wordy structures, rule class for, 76
Writing Problem window, 35
writing style
   analysis of, 30
   changing, 57–60
   comparison charts for, 52–54
   customized, 60–62
   house, 130
   ignoring rules for, 41
   new rules for, 118–120
   rule classes for, 74–76
   statistics for, 30, 49–52
   word usage profile for, 54–55

X

XyWrite, working with, 20

Selections from The SYBEX Library

WORD PROCESSING

The ABC's of Microsoft Word (Third Edition)
Alan R. Neibauer
461pp. Ref. 604-9
This is for the novice WORD user who wants to begin producing documents in the shortest time possible. Each chapter has short, easy-to-follow lessons for both keyboard and mouse, including all the basic editing, formatting and printing functions. Version 5.0.

The ABC's of WordPerfect
Alan R. Neibauer
239pp. Ref. 425-9
This basic introduction to WordPefect consists of short, step-by-step lessons—for new users who want to get going fast. Topics range from simple editing and formatting, to merging, sorting, macros, and more. Includes version 4.2

The ABC's of WordPerfect 5
Alan R. Neibauer
283pp. Ref. 504-2
This introduction explains the basics of desktop publishing with WordPerfect 5: editing, layout, formatting, printing, sorting, merging, and more. Readers are shown how to use WordPerfect 5's new features to produce great-looking reports.

The ABC's of WordPerfect 5.1
Alan R. Neibauer
352pp. Ref. 672-3
Neibauer's delightful writing style makes this clear tutorial an especially effective learning tool. Learn all about 5.1's new drop-down menus and mouse capabilities that reduce the tedious memorization of function keys.

The Complete Guide to MultiMate
Carol Holcomb Dreger
208pp. Ref. 229-9
This step-by-step tutorial is also an excellent reference guide to MultiMate features and uses. Topics include search/replace, library and merge functions, repagination, document defaults and more.

Encyclopedia WordPerfect 5.1
Greg Harvey
Kay Yarborough Nelson
1100pp. Ref. 676-6
This comprehensive, up-to-date WordPerfect reference is a must for beginning and experienced users alike. With complete, easy-to-find information on every WordPerfect feature and command—and it's organized by practical functions, with business users in mind.

Introduction to WordStar
Arthur Naiman
208pp. Ref. 134-9
This all time bestseller is an engaging first-time introduction to word processing as well as a complete guide to using WordStar—from basic editing to blocks, global searches, formatting, dot commands, SpellStar and MailMerge. Through Version 3.3.

Mastering Microsoft Word on the IBM PC (Fourth Edition)
Matthew Holtz
680pp. Ref. 597-2
This comprehensive, step-by-step guide details all the new desktop publishing developments in this versatile word processor, including details on editing, formatting, printing, and laser printing. Holtz uses sample business documents to dem-

onstrate the use of different fonts, graphics, and complex documents. Includes Fast Track speed notes. For Versions 4 and 5.

Mastering MultiMate Advantage II
Charles Ackerman
407pp. Ref. 482-8
This comprehensive tutorial covers all the capabilities of MultiMate, and highlights the differences between MultiMate Advantage II and previous versions—in pathway support, sorting, math, DOS access, using dBASE III, and more. With many practical examples, and a chapter on the On-File database.

Mastering WordPerfect
Susan Baake Kelly
435pp. Ref. 332-5
Step-by-step training from startup to mastery, featuring practical uses (form letters, newsletters and more), plus advanced topics such as document security and macro creation, sorting and columnar math. Through Version 4.2.

Mastering WordPerfect 5
Susan Baake Kelly
709pp. Ref. 500-X
The revised and expanded version of this definitive guide is now on WordPerfect 5 and covers wordprocessing and basic desktop publishing. As more than 200,000 readers of the original edition can attest, no tutorial approaches it for clarity and depth of treatment. Sorting, line drawing, and laser printing included.

Mastering WordPerfect 5.1
Alan Simpson
1050pp. Ref. 670-7
The ultimate guide for the WordPerfect user. Alan Simpson, the "master communicator," puts you in charge of the latest features of 5.1: new dropdown menus and mouse capabilities, along with the desktop publishing, macro programming, and file conversion functions that have made WordPerfect the most popular word processing program on the market.

Mastering WordStar Release 5.5
Greg Harvey
David J. Clark
450pp. Ref. 491-7
This book is the ultimate reference book for the newest version of WordStar. Readers may use Mastering to look up any word processing function, including the new Version 5 and 5.5 features and enhancements, and find detailed instructions for fundamental to advanced operations.

Microsoft Word Instant Reference for the IBM PC
Matthew Holtz
266pp. Ref. 692-8
Turn here for fast, easy access to concise information on every command and feature of Microsoft Word version 5.0—for editing, formatting, merging, style sheets, macros, and more. With exact keystroke sequences, discussion of command options, and commonly-performed tasks.

Practical WordStar Uses
Julie Anne Arca
303pp. Ref. 107-1
A hands-on guide to WordStar and MailMerge applications, with solutions to comon problems and "recipes" for day-to-day tasks. Formatting, merge-printing and much more; plus a quick-reference command chart and notes on CP/M and PC-DOS. For Version 3.3.

Understanding Professional Write
Gerry Litton
400pp. Ref. 656-1
A complete guide to Professional Write that takes you from creating your first simple document, into a detailed description of all major aspects of the software. Special features place an emphasis on the use of different typestyles to create attractive documents as well as potential problems and suggestions on how to get around them.

Understanding WordStar 2000
David Kolodney
Thomas Blackadar
275pp. Ref. 554-9

This engaging, fast-paced series of tutorials covers everything from moving the cursor to print enhancements, format files, key glossaries, windows and MailMerge. With practical examples, and notes for former WordStar users.

Visual Guide to WordPerfect
Jeff Woodward
457pp. Ref. 591-3

This is a visual hands-on guide which is ideal for brand new users as the book shows each activity keystroke-by-keystroke. Clear illustrations of computer screen menus are included at every stage. Covers basic editing, formatting lines, paragraphs, and pages, using the block feature, footnotes, search and replace, and more. Through Version 5.

WordPerfect 5 Desktop Companion
SYBEX Ready Reference Series
Greg Harvey
Kay Yarborough Nelson
1006pp. Ref. 522-0

Desktop publishing features have been added to this compact encyclopedia. This title offers more detailed, cross-referenced entries on every software feature including page formatting and layout, laser printing and word processing macros. New users of WordPerfect, and those new to Version 5 and desktop publishing will find this easy to use for on-the-job help.

WordPerfect 5 Instant Reference
SYBEX Prompter Series
Greg Harvey
Kay Yarborough Nelson
316pp. Ref. 535-2, 4 3/4" × 8"

This pocket-sized reference has all the program commands for the powerful WordPerfect 5 organized alphabetically for quick access. Each command entry has the exact key sequence, any reveal codes, a list of available options, and option-by-option discussions.

WordPerfect 5.1 Instant Reference
Greg Harvey
Kay Yarborough Nelson
252pp. Ref. 674-X

Instant access to all features and commands of WordPerfect 5.0 and 5.1, highlighting the newest software features. Complete, alphabetical entries provide exact key sequences, codes and options, and step-by-step instructions for many important tasks.

WordPerfect 5.1 Macro Handbook
Kay Yarborough Nelson
532pp. Ref. 687-1

Help yourself to over 150 ready-made macros for WordPerfect versions 5.0 and 5.1. This complete tutorial guide to creating and using work-saving macros is a must for every serious WordPerfect user. Hands-on lessons show you exactly how to record and use your first simple macros—then build to sophisticated skills.

WordPerfect 5.1 Tips and Tricks (Fourth Edition)
Alan R. Neibauer
675pp. Ref. 681-2

This new edition is a real timesaver. For on-the-job guidance and creative new uses, this title covers all versions of WordPerfect up to and including 5.1—streamlining documents, automating with macros, new print enhancements, and more.

WordStar Instant Reference
SYBEX Prompter Series
David J. Clark
314pp. Ref. 543-3, 4 3/4" × 8"

This quick reference provides reminders on the use of the editing, formatting, mailmerge, and document processing commands available through WordStar 4 and 5. Operations are organized alphabetically for easy access. The text includes a survey of the menu system and instructions for installing and customizing WordStar.

Text Editing Commands on the Error Detection Screen

Key	Function
Del	Deletes the character at the cursor.
Backspace	Deletes the character to left of the cursor.
↑	Moves the cursor up one line.
↓	Moves the cursor down one line.
←	Moves the cursor left one character.
→	Moves the cursor right one character.
Ctrl-←	Moves the cursor left one word.
Ctrl-→	Moves the cursor right one word.
Ctrl-L	Deletes the line.
Ins	Toggles between Insert and Overtype mode.